# Better to Be Pissed Off Than Pissed On

# Better to Be Pissed Off Than Pissed On

## (A Collection of Rants, Truths, and Other Inconvenient Realities)

Gregory Jerman

**Cinnamon
Curl Press**

Copyright © 2026 by Gregory Jerman
All rights reserved.

No part of this book may be reproduced, distributed, or transmitted in any form or by any means, including photocopying, recording, or other electronic or mechanical methods, without the prior written permission of the copyright holder, except in the case of brief quotations embodied in critical reviews and certain other noncommercial uses permitted by copyright law.

**ISBN:** 979-8-218-89285-2

**Library of Congress Control Number:** 2026902651

Published by **Cinnamon Curl Press**
Sacramento, California

This is a work of humor and commentary based on real-life experiences and observations. Some names and identifying details have been changed, and certain events may be condensed or combined for readability.

All trademarks and registered trademarks are the property of their respective owners. References to companies, products, and their services are used for identification and commentary only and do not imply endorsement or affiliation.

**First Edition**

Printed in the United States of America

For my wife and daughters,
Who put up with me long enough for this book to exist,
You deserve a medal…or at least a nap.

# Table of Contents

**INTRO - The Philosophy of Being Pissed Off**.....................1
*Why anger is rational, honest, and sometimes the only reasonable reaction to a stupid world.*

**PART I - The World Is Nuts**............................................11
*A guided tour of everything wrong with society, culture, and the systems that supposedly keep things running.*

1. People Have Forgotten How to Think..................................12
*Critical thinking, common sense, and the extinction of logic.*

2. Everyone's Offended Until It's Time to Be Accountable.............25
*Performative outrage, cancel culture, and the allergy to responsibility.*

3. Politics and Incompetence..............................................42
*How leadership lost the plot, and why both sides drive sane people insane.*

4. Bureaucracy: The Art of Doing Nothing Slowly......................60
*Red tape, pointless processes, and government systems that barely function.*

5. Economics and Inequality...............................................78
*Why working harder means less, and how the system is rigged with a smile.*

6. Healthcare: Where Hope Goes to Die..................................92
*A tour of America's medical maze - overpriced, understaffed, and overcomplicated.*

7. Social Media Made Everyone Worse...................................100
*The dopamine casino, misinformation, and the rise of the professionally outraged.*

8. Technology Was Supposed to Help… and It Made Everything Worse.........................................................................107
*Smart devices, dumb results, and the illusion of progress.*

9. Corporations Doing Dumb Shit..........................................122
*Customer "service," bloated policies, and decisions made by people who've never met reality.*

10. Celebrities and the Cult of Forced Opinions........................136
*How fame somehow turned into a PhD in everything.*

11. Why America Is Basically a Daily Headache.........................147
*Everything above, blended into one giant societal migraine.*

**PART II - Daily Life: A Comedy of Frustrations**...............154
*The everyday torture we all endure but rarely talk about without swearing.*

12. Neighbors: Proof That Hell Is Real....................................155
*Loud ones, nosey ones, HOA enforcers, and the ones who make you consider moving.*

13. HOA Rules and Other Forms of Petty Tyranny.....................161
*The tiny dictators who care more about your trash cans than world peace.*

14. Traffic: A Social Experiment Gone Wrong..........................170
*Merging, tailgating, left-lane squatters - and why every road becomes a war zone.*

15. Airports and Airlines: The Ninth Circle of Hell....................180
*Delayed flights, shrinking seats, outrageous fees, and people who forget how lines work.*

16. Workplace Nonsense and Other Corporate Fairy Tales...........188
*Meetings that should've been emails, HR buzzwords, and dumb policies no one follows.*

17. Five-Minute Tasks That Somehow Take Two Hours............199
*The cable company, the post office, "quick" errands, and the cruel time warp of adulthood.*

18. The DMV: Bureaucratic Torture With Fluorescent Lighting.....209
*A special chapter for a special kind of suffering.*

19. Part-Time Dads and the Parenthood Participation Trophy.......217
*Some dads act like showing up twice a month makes them Father of the Year.*

20. Holiday Creep: When Companies Celebrate Christmas in October......................................................................227
*I can't buy Halloween candy anymore without tripping over Santa Claus.*

21. Adults Who Shouldn't Be Adults........................................236
*Some people aren't adults. They're just tall children with debit cards.*

22. Influencers: The New Used-Car Salesmen..........................247
*If an influencer tells you something's life-changing, check who's paying them first.*

23. People Who Overshare on Social Media............................258
*Some people would livestream their own arrest if they had enough followers.*

24. Why Customer Loyalty Programs Are Scams......................270
*If you need my zip code, phone number, birthday, and mother's maiden name for a $1 discount, it's not a reward - it's surveillance.*

25. Every Company Wants Me to Take a Damn Survey...............279
*Because not every purchase requires a performance review.*

26. The Death of Privacy and Why Everyone Seems Fine With It.....287
*We're one software update away from our microwaves asking for consent to store cookies."*

v

**PART III - Things That Shouldn't Piss Me Off... But Totally Do**..................................................................................298
*Minor annoyances that feel like personal attacks.*

27. People Who Can't Park.................................................299
*Diagonal drivers, space hogs, and the ones who somehow park worse with backup cameras.*

28. Adults Who Microwave Fish in Public................................311
*Workplace war crimes and crimes against humanity.*

29. Small Talk: I Hate It Here............................................319
*Weather updates, forced smiles, and conversations that drain your will to live.*

30. Unsolicited Advice and Other Forms of Torture....................328
*People who know everything - except when to shut up.*

31. Why I Don't Trust Anyone Who Says "Circle Back"...............337
*Corporate-speak, empty phrases, and why buzzwords make everything worse.*

32. Cheaters: The Art of Getting Ahead Without Earning It..........344
*Cheaters break rules; the rest of us pay the bill.*

**PART IV - What We Can Actually Do About It**.....................352
*Because being pissed off is valid - but staying pissed off forever will kill you.*

33. How Not to Lose Your Mind in a Ridiculous World................353
*Sanity strategies for modern chaos.*

34. Stoicism for Pissed-Off People......................................362
*Philosophy for those who'd rather punch a wall.*

35. Choosing Your Battles (Even When You Want to Fight All of Them).......................................................................367
*When to speak up, when to walk away, and when to pretend you didn't hear anything.*

36. Finding Humor in the Absurd..........................................376
*Laughing so you don't scream.*

37. The Surprisingly Rewarding Art of Not Giving a Damn...........386
*Freedom, boundaries, and mastering the "nope" lifestyle.*

**CONCLUSION - You're Not Wrong for Being Pissed Off**...395
*You're not wrong - just living in a ridiculous world and reacting.*

# INTRO - The Philosophy of Being Pissed Off

There's a strange thing that happens in this country whenever someone admits they're pissed off: people act like it's an emotional defect. Like irritation is some contagious disease we're all expected to hide under a polite smile and a cheery "No worries!" while everything around us catches fire.

But the truth is simple:

Being pissed off is one of the last honest reactions we have left.
Being pissed off means you're awake.
It means you're paying attention.
It means the world hasn't numbed you into that dazed "Everything's fine" trance slapped across half the population.

Somewhere along the way, society decided the "appropriate" response to frustration is to pretend you're not frustrated. You're supposed to breathe deeply, count to ten, drink herbal tea, and journal your emotions like you're training for a mindfulness decathlon.

Meanwhile:

your internet bill just went up again,
the DMV misplaced your paperwork (again),
Walmart has Christmas trees out in September,
and your neighbor is leaf-blowing at 6:15 a.m.

But sure - tell me more about deep breathing.

The truth is, there's never been a better time to be pissed off.
Not violent.

Not unhinged.
Not ranting into the void in a bathrobe on your front lawn.
Just reasonably, rationally pissed - the kind that comes from watching the parade of nonsense and thinking:

*Are we all seeing the same world, or did I accidentally tune into a knockoff simulation where the developers quit halfway through?*

People love to preach positivity.
"Choose joy."
"Be grateful."
"Smile through it!"

They say this while doing something irritating.

Nobody talks about the value of being irritated.
Nobody admits that sometimes being pissed off is the only sane reaction to an insane world.

Because let's be honest: half the time, the world behaves like a toddler with car keys.
The other half, it behaves like a corporation with a marketing department.

And that's why this book exists - not to make you angry, not to teach you to hate everything, not to turn you into a miserable sack of complaints.
But to finally say out loud the thing everyone secretly feels:

Sometimes life is easier to handle when you laugh at how stupid everything is.

And make no mistake - there's plenty of stupidity to choose from.

This is why we can't have nice things.

# The First Time I Realized the World Cheats

Back in the late 1990s, I was a baseball fan. And by "a baseball fan," I don't mean I casually knew the difference between a shortstop and a barstool. I mean I *was* baseball - lived it, breathed it, and probably would've bled pine tar if you cut me open.

Then the steroid scandal hit.

America's wholesome pastime suddenly looked less like *Field of Dreams* and more like *Maury: You Are Not the Father.*
My first love cheated on me.

Lied to me.

For years.

The betrayal felt personal - like being emotionally sucker-punched by someone you worshipped.

So I did the only thing I could:
I vented.
I ranted.
I wrote.

Somewhere in that hormonal storm of outrage, this book took its first breath.

But here's the part I didn't understand until much later:

Baseball wasn't the anomaly.
It was just the opening act.
The warm-up band for the main show: everything else.

People cheat at everything - taxes, relationships, résumés, reality.

Companies cheat customers.
Politicians cheat the public.
Half the world is juicing something: their stats, their stories, their social media personas.

Fast-forward a couple decades.

I'm still pissed - just not about back-acne-to-home-run ratios. Now it's the real-world stupidity, hypocrisy, incompetence, and general "what-the-hell-is-wrong-with-people" factor that gets worse every year.

So I'm still venting.
Still ranting.
Still writing.
Still trying to keep my arteries from turning into artisanal concrete.

And that's where this book begins - not with baseball, but with the realization that life constantly gives you reasons to be pissed off... and somehow, laughing about it keeps you alive a little longer.

## Why Being Pissed Off Makes Sense

Let's start with the obvious: there is nothing irrational about being frustrated by the world we live in.
If anything, what's *irrational* is how many people walk around unfazed by the absurdity shoved in their faces daily.

Think about the average week:

Someone cuts you off and then flips **you** off.
You shout "AGENT!" into a robot for 17 minutes.
A celebrity posts a political essay after reading half a Wikipedia page.
Your boss schedules a meeting to "touch base" about absolutely nothing.

You buy a $5 item and get three survey emails demanding emotional feedback.

You try to buy Halloween candy in October and a Christmas elf falls into your cart.

And when you show even a flicker of irritation, someone chirps, "Hey, lighten up!"

Lighten up?

Buddy, if I lighten up any further, I'll float into the atmosphere like a pissed-off balloon.

Being pissed off doesn't mean you're negative.
It means you have standards.
It means you're not desensitized to nonsense.
It means you're still emotionally alive enough to notice when something is stupid.

There's a difference between being petty angry and being righteously pissed.

Petty angry is being mad at:
a pen that quits for half a second,
someone breathing too loudly,
a fork falling off the counter,
your phone autocorrecting "ducking."

We've all been there.

But righteously pissed is different:

Why do people refuse to use turn signals like the bulb costs $800?
Why does the DMV operate like a psychological endurance test?
Why does every company announce price hikes as "an exciting update"?

Why are influencers acting like experts when they barely mastered inhaling?
Why does every office have one person microwaving fish at 11 a.m.?

This is the stuff that unites us all.

If you've ever looked at the world and thought, *Am I the only one who sees how ridiculous this is?*

You're my people.

This is why we can't have nice things.

## What This Book Is Not

This is not:
a rage manifesto,
a political lecture,
a doom-scroll in paperback,
or a self-help manual pretending your problems can be solved with sunrise yoga and positive vibes.

You will not find affirmations here.
You will not find "eight steps to inner peace."
You will not find exercises about visualizing abundance.

## What This Book Is

This book is one long exhale.

It's the release valve for modern life.
Permission to admit that yes, things annoy the hell out of you - and that's normal.

Because we need more honesty.

We need more humor.
We need more people willing to point at the obvious and say:

"This is stupid. Why are we accepting it?"

And that brings us to Part I.

But before we dive into society's biggest nonsense pile, let's be very clear:

You're not imagining it.
The world *really is* getting dumber.

## The Daily Test of Sanity

Modern life gives you 14 irritations before breakfast:

Your phone shouts notifications you don't care about.
Your email inbox is a digital junkyard.
Your coffee maker accuses you of crimes.
Your car lectures you about tire pressure like a disappointed parent.

By the time you scroll social media, you're not angry at anything specific - you're angry at *everything*.

Your baseline becomes "mildly irritated," like a smoke detector that chirps once every 47 seconds.

Not enough to ruin your life…
but enough to remind you that the world is annoying on purpose.

## The Lie of Staying Positive

People think negativity is a moral failing.

They call frustration "toxic."
They call boundaries "selfish."
They call honesty "negative energy."

Meanwhile, you're expected to smile politely while corporations drain your wallet, waste your time, and send you emails that begin with "We're excited to share…" (Nothing exciting has ever followed that sentence.)

Being pissed off isn't negativity.
It's awareness.

And it's the refusal to be gaslit into pretending nonsense is normal.

## You're Not Imagining It - The World Really Is Chaotic

Systems are worse.
Customer service is worse.
Rules are dumber.
Technology is more invasive.
People are less self-aware.
Corporations think you're a subscription-based organism.

You're not overreacting.
You're reacting appropriately.

And that's why this book exists: for people who see the cracks and are tired of pretending not to.

This isn't a book about fixing the world.
It's about recognizing it clearly enough to stop blaming yourself for being frustrated by it.

## Why We Need Humor

You can't survive the modern world on serenity alone.

You need humor - real humor.
Not the forced "choose happiness" kind.
The kind that turns absurdity into perspective.
The kind that keeps you sane enough not to snap at a self-checkout robot.

Being pissed off is easier when you can laugh about the absurdity instead of drowning in it.

That's the whole point of this book:
Weaponize frustration.
Turn nonsense into comedy.
Stay sane by refusing to pretend the world isn't stupid.

## The One Rule of Rational Anger

Don't let the world turn you into an asshole.

Let it piss you off just enough to stay awake.

That's the lane this book lives in - the middle ground where frustration, humor, honesty, and perspective all roll their eyes in unison.

If that's you?

You're home.

# Where We're Headed

As irritating as daily life is, it's nothing compared to the large-scale circus we call society.

People aren't thinking.
Systems aren't working.
Everyone's pretending.
Everything's absurd.

So buckle up and get ready for **Part I: The World Is Nuts.**

If you're already annoyed, perfect.
If you're not annoyed yet, give me five pages - I promise you will be.

And when you are?

You'll finally know you're in the right place.

**PART I - THE WORLD IS NUTS**
A tour of societal dysfunction, hypocrisy, and everyday insanity.

# CHAPTER 1 - People Have Forgotten How to Think

There was a time - not that long ago - when thinking was considered a basic function of being alive. People used to have ideas, form opinions after hearing both sides, ask questions, examine evidence, and occasionally even change their minds.

Now?

Thinking has gone the way of Blockbuster: technically not dead, but hanging on by a thread while everyone else pretends there's no need for it anymore.

Modern society has replaced thinking with a cocktail of:
gut reactions,
emotions,
blind tribalism,
hashtags,
internet confidence,
and the intellectual curiosity of a potato.

Somewhere along the line, common sense - once the backbone of functional adulthood - died quietly in a ditch while the rest of the world was scrolling TikTok.

And nobody noticed.

# The Death of Common Sense

There used to be rules - not official ones, just universal truths - that helped society function.

Things like:
"Look both ways before crossing the street."
"Maybe don't provoke the angry dog."
"If something smells like death, maybe don't eat it."
"If you don't know the answer, admit it."
"If a stranger on the internet tells you to 'try this trick doctors hate,' don't."

Common sense used to be the foundation of survival.

But modern society has turned common sense into a "controversial opinion."

You can't even say something logical without someone pulling out their phone and Googling an argument against it.

We went from a world where a fool was obvious, to a world where fools are celebrated as "authentic personalities."

We're living in a golden age of people who proudly declare:

"I don't care what the facts say, this is how I FEEL."

That sentence alone should qualify you for a supervised adult chaperone.

Now, look - I'm not saying everyone used to be smart. Dumb people have always existed. But in the past, dumb people had the decency to keep their dumbness quiet.

They stayed silent.
They stayed humble.
They stayed in the background, quietly confused but harmless.

Now?

Dumb people have confidence.
Dumb people have platforms.
Dumb people have followings.
Dumb people have podcasts.

Once upon a time, stupidity was a limitation.

Now it's a brand.

This is why we can't have nice things.

## People Believe Memes More Than Facts

I wish this was an exaggeration, but people genuinely treat memes like Biblical scripture.

A meme can say:
"Spiders crawl into your mouth 14 times a night."
"Carrots cure depression."
"Everything you believe is wrong; share this to save the world."

And people will believe it with zero hesitation.

Memes require no nuance, no thought, no analysis - and that's exactly why they win.

They're spoon-fed certainty for people who can't be bothered to chew.

Facts?

Those require effort.
Time.
Reading.
Comprehension.

Sometimes even admitting you were wrong - and that's the cardinal sin of the digital age.

Memes don't ask you to be a better person.

They ask you to giggle and press "Share."

And somehow, "Share" has replaced "Think."

We laugh, but it's genuinely frightening how many people build their entire worldview out of images made by anonymous teenagers doing it for clout.

## Outrage-Driven Thinking vs. Logic

One of the biggest markers of society's intellectual decline is that feelings now outrank logic.

It doesn't matter if something is true - it only matters how it makes people feel.

If a statement makes someone uncomfortable, we're expected to pretend it's invalid.
If an idea challenges someone's worldview, they melt down like a cheap candle in a sauna.

We've created a society where:
hurt feelings = wrong,
calm logic = aggressive,

disagreement = violence,
a differing opinion = "attacking my identity."

How can anyone think when every conversation is a minefield?

People used to debate ideas.

Now they debate emotions.

And emotions aren't arguments - they're reactions.

But online, everyone acts like their feelings are definitive evidence:

"I feel offended, therefore you're wrong."

No.

You're not wrong because someone feels offended.

You're wrong when your argument makes no sense - and that usually happens long before feelings enter the equation.

## Masks, Conspiracy Theories, and the Public Meltdown

Nothing exposed society's thinking crisis quite like the last round of healthcare debates.

Suddenly, half the population who'd never read anything more complex than a shampoo bottle became overnight experts in:
virology,
immunology,
statistics,
constitutional law,
public health,

airborne particle behavior.

You had people saying:

"I did my research."

Which meant:
they watched a YouTube video,
they read a meme,
they skimmed a Reddit thread,
or they heard their cousin's neighbor rant over barbecue.

It was a global masterclass in how fast misinformation spreads.

You could show someone peer-reviewed studies, global consensus, and the opinions of experts with 30-year careers...

...and they'd respond with:

"Nah. Doesn't feel right."

We reached a point where people couldn't even agree on:
what a virus is,
how it spreads,
whether washing hands is overrated,
or whether the moon landing was staged by Costco's marketing department (I wish that last one was a joke).

And all of this happened publicly.
In real time.
On social media.
With millions watching.

It was like watching society take a collective IQ test - and fail spectacularly.

# Social Media: Where Logic Goes to Die

Social media didn't make people dumb - it simply revealed how many people were already dumb and gave them a megaphone.

It's the digital Wild West, filled with:
bad takes,
emotional outbursts,
half-thoughts,
keyboard warriors,
trolls with too much free time,
MLM moms trying to recruit you into "clean living,"
unhinged life coaches who use phrases like "vibrational frequency" unironically.

The problem isn't disagreement - it's the complete inability to discuss anything.

Look at any comment section:
people talk past each other,
nobody reads,
everyone reacts,
context doesn't exist,
nuance died in 2010.

You'll see arguments where both sides are wrong, neither side knows they're wrong, and everyone is furious.

The internet didn't destroy logic.

It just made logic optional.

# The Rise of Google Experts

Nothing encapsulates the death of thinking like the modern Google expert.

These are people who open Google, type five words, and suddenly believe they're the reincarnation of Einstein.

They love saying:
"I've done my research."
"The science is unclear."
"Experts are divided."
"Here's what the data suggests…" (they have no data)

Google didn't empower people - it inflated their confidence.

Having access to information is not the same as understanding it.
Being able to find answers is not the same as knowing what they mean.
Reading a Wikipedia article is not the same as being educated.

If Google experts ever had to operate without internet access, they'd collapse like a house made of soggy cardboard.

I knew society had officially tapped out of thinking when I pulled into a fast-food drive-thru and watched a guy sitting at the menu board arguing with the speaker because he couldn't grasp the concept of "repeat your order."

The employee said, "Sir, can you repeat that?"
The man yelled, "I JUST SAID IT!"

Yes.
That was the problem.
You said it.
She didn't hear it.

This is how communication works - you speak, the other person hears.

He got so mad he pulled up to the window and said, "Your speaker's broken."

The employee calmly replied, "No sir, your window was rolled up."

He argued with a speaker for two minutes because he couldn't figure out that talking through closed glass is ineffective.

And that's when it hit me:

People aren't stupid because they lack intelligence - they're stupid because they've stopped using it.

This is why we can't have nice things.

## Nobody Can Disagree Without Melting Down

Once upon a time, disagreements sounded like this:

Person A: "I think the movie was good."
Person B: "I disagree."
Person A: "Fair enough."

End of discussion.

Now disagreements sound like this:

Person A: "I think the movie was good."
Person B: "Wow. Typical. You would say that. Unbelievable."
Person A: "What?"
Person B: "You're ignorant. Blocked."

People treat opposing opinions like personal betrayals.

We've created a culture where fragility is mistaken for conviction.

People are emotionally flammable.

One spark and BOOM - explosion.

And this isn't limited to politics.

People will meltdown over:
pizza toppings,
celebrity gossip,
cats vs. dogs,
whether pineapple belongs anywhere near an oven,
which version of *The Office* is better.

There's no middle ground.
No nuance.
No curiosity.

Just:
rage,
defensiveness,
projection,
blocks,
vague threats,
and people "going private for my mental health."

We have an entire society composed of adults who handle disagreements with the maturity of a toddler throwing a sippy cup.

# A Small List of Things That Used to Require Thought (But Now Cause Chaos)

Here are a few tasks that absolutely should not require the mental equivalent of a SWAT team:

**Using a turn signal**
The easiest task in driving.
Yet half the population treats it like a national secret.

**Reading a menu**
Somehow requires five clarification questions, two substitutions, and a TED Talk.

**Following "Line Starts Here" signs**
People still wander around like confused goats.

**Being on time**
Not early.
Not perfect.
Just not 20 minutes late every time.

**Understanding sarcasm**
We live in the most sarcastic era in human history and people still reply,
"Wait... really?"

**Returning a shopping cart**
The ultimate test of basic decency - and so many people fail it.

**Distinguishing news from opinion**
A line that has apparently been erased, blurred, smudged, or eaten.

**Charging their phone before leaving the house**
Adults walking around at 2% battery like they live dangerously.

**Knowing when to stop talking**
A lost art.

**Accepting that sometimes other people know more than you**
Now considered "elitism."

---

# Why This Chapter Matters

This chapter is more than a rant - it's the backbone of the entire book.

Every topic in the remaining chapters traces back to one central problem:

People aren't thinking.

That's why:
traffic sucks,
parenting is out of control,
influencers have power,
celebrities lecture us,
customer service is a wasteland,
cheaters are everywhere,
privacy is dead,
society is confused,
everyday tasks feel harder,
people treat feelings as truth,
and the world feels stupider every year.

When thinking collapses, everything collapses with it.

Frustration becomes the default emotional setting.
Annoyance becomes the background noise of adulthood.

And being pissed off isn't an overreaction -
it's a completely rational response to an irrational world.

Welcome to Chapter 1.

The world has forgotten how to think.
And now we get to explore everything that happened because of it.

# CHAPTER 2 - Everyone's Offended Until It's Time to Be Accountable

We are living in the golden age of outrage.

Not justified outrage.
Not righteous anger.
Not the kind of fury that stops injustice or inspires real reform.

I'm talking about hobby-level outrage - the recreational kind practiced by people who have unlimited screen time and extremely limited self-awareness.

Being offended isn't a reaction anymore.
It's a lifestyle.
A movement.
A hobby.
A full-blown identity.

You can't say anything without someone clutching their emotional pearls and announcing that what you said was:
insensitive,
problematic,
harmful,
emotionally violent,
psychologically disruptive,
or (my favorite) "deeply triggering."

Some folks treat their emotional sensitivity like it's a rare medical condition that we're all required to accommodate.

It used to be that if something offended you, you shrugged, moved on, or simply avoided it.

Now, being offended is a competitive sport where the goal is to:
react first,
react loudest,
react most dramatically,
and get the most digital applause for it.

Welcome to modern society, where everyone's offended right up until someone asks them to look in the mirror.

## Performative Outrage as Currency

Somewhere along the line, outrage became a form of social currency.

It's the digital version of a gym membership: everyone brags about having it, but only a few actually use it for anything meaningful.

The pattern is always the same:
Someone says something that mildly annoys a stranger with Wi-Fi.
That stranger publicly declares themselves offended.
Their followers rally around them like they're leading a civil rights movement because someone made a joke about oat milk.
BOOM - instant validation.

Being offended online gets attention.
Attention gets influence.
Influence gets dopamine.

It's emotional inflation - the more you react, the more "important" you feel.

People are addicted to outrage because it's:

easy,
free,
consequence-free,
and gives temporary meaning to people who otherwise have none.

It's never about the issue.

It's about the moment.

The moment of power.

The moment of validation.

The moment of "Look at me, I'm morally enlightened."

## The Guy Who Got Offended at a Weather Forecast

I once saw a man online get offended at a weather forecast.

Not even a political forecast.

Just the weather.

The meteorologist said,

"We're expecting a lot of sunshine this weekend."

And the guy commented:

"Wow. Way to rub it in for those of us who have to work Saturdays."

Imagine being so emotionally fragile that the sun offends you.

This is what we're dealing with now.

People are looking for reasons to get upset - and when they can't find any, they manufacture them.

This is why we can't have nice things.

## People Who Demand Accountability but Don't Practice It

If performative outrage is the disease, lack of accountability is the symptom.

We live in a world where people scream for accountability like they're auditioning for a courtroom drama - yet when it's their turn to be accountable?

Suddenly nobody knows what accountability means.

People love accountability as long as:
they're not involved,
it doesn't affect them,
it doesn't require them to change,
it doesn't force them to admit they screwed up.

It's always:

"People need to do better!"

…until the spotlight turns.

Then it becomes:
"Well, there's more to the story…"
"You don't know what I'm going through."
"I'm doing my best."
"It was taken out of context."

"Why are you attacking me?"

People weaponize accountability until someone tries to use it on them.

It's like watching someone cheer for a speeding ticket - until they get pulled over.

## The Woman Who Demanded an Apology for Something She Did

I once knew a woman who insisted someone owed her an apology for something she did.

She double-booked a lunch date.
She mixed up the time.
She showed up late.
She blamed traffic.
She blamed "the universe."

Then she said:

"Honestly, you should apologize for making me feel bad about being late."

She didn't want forgiveness.

She wanted permission to be irresponsible without consequences.

This is basically the mission statement of modern outrage culture.

## Being Offended as a Personality

Some people don't have hobbies.

They have grievances.

You know the type:
They get offended when a barista gets their name wrong.
They get offended when a cashier says "Have a good day" with the wrong tone.
They get offended when they see someone wearing a shirt they personally dislike.
They get offended when a comedian makes a joke that wasn't handcrafted to their specific sensitivities.

These people treat their emotional sensitivities like a form of activism.

Their personality revolves around:
correcting people,
exposing things,
calling out behavior,
posting "awareness,"
publicly venting.

They have the emotional stability of an overturned shopping cart and the self-awareness of a houseplant.

Being offended isn't something that happens to them.
It's something they seek out - like it's part of their morning routine.

Coffee.
Scroll.
Look for something to get mad about.
Repeat.

# The Woman at the Restaurant

I once saw a woman get offended at a restaurant because the waiter said:

"Enjoy your meal."

She turned to her friend and said:

"That's so controlling. Who is he to tell me how to enjoy my food?"

Lady…

It's a greeting, not a hostage negotiation.

Some people treat basic politeness as an emotional attack.

This is why we can't have nice things.

# The Court of Public Opinion Has Replaced Rational Discussion

We don't resolve conflicts anymore.

We televise them.

Rational discussion has been replaced by:
screenshot trials,
mob justice,
public shaming,
witch hunts,
narrative manipulation,
emotional storytelling.

There's no:
searching for the truth,
fact-checking,
waiting for context,
allowing people to clarify,
giving anyone a chance to explain.

The entire system now works like this:
Someone posts a clip.
Someone overreacts.
Everyone else overreacts to that overreaction.
A dogpile forms.
The person in question tries to explain.
The mob doesn't care.
The story gets old.
Everyone moves on to the next target.

It's digital gladiatorial combat - but instead of swords, we use tweets, out-of-context clips, and bad-faith interpretations.

## The Man Who Overreacted to a Parking Lot Video

There was a viral video where a guy parked badly at a grocery store.

That's it.

Bad parking.

Someone filmed it and uploaded the video.

Within minutes, thousands of people were in the comments screaming things like:
"This man should lose his license!"
"JAIL."

"He's a danger to society."

It was just a dude who parked crooked.

He wasn't running over pedestrians.
He wasn't committing a felony.
He wasn't evading the IRS.

He just didn't straighten his wheels.

But the mob was foaming at the mouth, demanding justice like he'd committed war crimes.

This is the Court of Public Opinion in a nutshell:

Regular people doing regular dumb things treated like capital offenses.

## Top 20 Things People Get Offended By for Absolutely No Reason

**Weather**
Too hot? Offended.
Too cold? Offended.
Rain? Personally attacked.
Sunshine? "Wow, must be nice."

**Being told "Good morning"**
Apparently some people wake up ready for psychological combat.

**Someone having a different coffee order**
"What do you mean you don't drink oat milk? Bigot."

**Cashiers saying "Enjoy your day"**
"How dare you pressure me to enjoy anything."

**Traffic laws being enforced**
"HOW DARE YOU GIVE ME A TICKET FOR SOMETHING I 100% DID."

**Someone getting in line before them (even though they weren't there yet)**
Teleportation is now a constitutional right.

**People eating food 'incorrectly'**
Fork in the wrong hand? Offended.
Ketchup on a hot dog? Call 911.

**The existence of pineapple on pizza**
Not liking it? Fine.
Acting like it violates the Geneva Convention? Unhinged.

**Someone saying "no worries"**
Apparently this phrase triggers flashbacks of childhood trauma for some people.

**Someone not responding instantly to a text**
"Wow, I guess I'm not a priority."
You're right. You're not.

**Dogs barking**
Yes. How dare a mammal communicate using the exact noise it evolved to make.

**Babies crying**
"I can't believe that baby is crying. How inconsiderate of its developing nervous system."

**Someone else's happiness**
Nothing makes miserable people angrier than seeing someone else having a good day.

**Mild inconvenience**
If the Starbucks line is more than 4 minutes long, some people lose the will to live.

**Being asked to show basic manners**
"Hey, can you please not scream on speakerphone in the grocery store?"
"WOW. Attacked."

**People saying "calm down"**
This one is fair.
Nobody has ever calmed down from being told to calm down.
Still funny, though.

**Someone having a different opinion**
Not even a controversial opinion - ANY opinion.
"What do you mean you like the other Marvel movie?"

**The phrase "We're out of stock."**
Retail workers say this and immediately enter the witness protection program.

**Other people breathing 'too loudly'**
The #1 cause of quiet workplace hatred.

**The existence of other humans**
Some people walk around offended simply because society requires them to interact with other people.

# Outrage Whiplash - Yesterday's Villain Is Tomorrow's Hero

One of the funniest, dumbest phenomena of modern society is how outrage flips.

Someone gets hated on Monday.
Tweeted about on Tuesday.
Cancelled on Wednesday.
Semi-forgiven on Thursday.
And by Friday they're inspirational.

The cycle is so stupid you could set your watch to it.

It goes like this:
Someone makes a mistake.
Mob attacks.
The person disappears for 48 hours.
Issues a notes-app apology.
Posts a tearful video talking about "growth."
Reposts inspirational quotes.
Says they're "focusing on mental health."
Random people start defending them again.
The cycle resets when someone else becomes the target.

It's outrage whiplash.

No consistency.
No standards.
No logic.

Just emotional chaos.

## Mock Apologies Nobody Believes

Let's take a moment to appreciate the pure comedy gold of modern apologies.

Every apology now reads like it was written by a **PR** team using AI on a 12-second timer.

Here's what they usually look like:

**Apology Style #1 - The Notes App Special**
Straight from the iPhone, grayscale filter, emotionless font.

"I'm sorry if anyone was offended."

Translation:
"I'm not sorry. You're sensitive."

**Apology Style #2 - The Tearful Video**
Shot from a depressing angle, wearing a hoodie, wiping fake tears.

"This has been the hardest time of my life."

Translation:
"This has been the hardest week of my social media life."

**Apology Style #3 - The Spiritual Awakening**
Usually begins with:

"I've done a lot of soul searching."

Translation:
"I've done a lot of googling to figure out how to get people off my back."

**Apology Style #4 - The Blame-Shift Apology**

"I was in a dark place."
"I didn't feel supported."
"Other people influenced me."

Translation:
"I take full responsibility... for everyone else's actions."

**Apology Style #5 - The Redemption Tour**
New haircut.
All-white outfit.
Suddenly talking about "growth."
Appearing on a podcast titled something like *Growth, Allegedly*.

It's a PR baptism.

## People Love Holding Others to Standards They Don't Live By

This section could be its own chapter.

Hell, it could be its own book.

People demand perfection from:
celebrities,
influencers,
politicians,
bosses,
teachers,
coworkers.

But refuse to apply that same perfection to themselves.

They talk about:
accountability,
integrity,
authenticity,
empathy,
responsibility…

…while simultaneously:
cutting people off in traffic,
cheating on partners,

lying to friends,
ignoring their kids,
stealing office supplies,
gossiping,
ditching commitments,
blaming others,
sabotaging coworkers,
manipulating relationships.

It's hypocrisy so thick you could spread it on toast.

## Why Outrage Feels Good (Even When It's Fake)

Psychologists say outrage gives people a sense of:
control,
identity,
connection,
excitement,
purpose.

In a world where people feel lost, bored, lonely, and powerless, outrage becomes a convenient emotional weapon.

It's the emotional equivalent of scratching a mosquito bite - satisfying in the moment, destructive in the long term.

Outrage lets people:
avoid introspection,
avoid growth,
avoid responsibility,
distract themselves,
get attention,
feel moral.

It's emotional fast food.

It tastes good.
It's easy.
It's cheap.

And it leaves you feeling worse afterward.

## The Guy Who Apologized for Nothing

I once saw a man apologize for standing in line.

He wasn't doing anything wrong.

He was just standing there, minding his business, waiting his turn.

Someone bumped into him and said:

"Watch it!"

And he replied:

"Oh my god, I'm so sorry, I didn't mean… "

He was apologizing for existing.

That's what happens when society gets addicted to outrage:
innocent people apologize automatically,
guilty people never apologize at all.

The entire emotional economy collapses.

This is why we can't have nice things.

# Why This Chapter Matters

This chapter explains the emotional climate we're all forced to live in.

In a world where:
people get offended at weather,
accountability is optional,
outrage is recreational,
hypocrisy is normal,
apologies are performance art.

...you end up with a society overflowing with tension, confusion, and stupidity.

And guess who gets stuck navigating it?

You.
Me.
Everyone with common sense.
Everyone who isn't emotionally allergic to reality.

This book is about the daily frustrations of modern life - and none of those frustrations make sense without understanding the environment they grow in.

When people stop thinking, stop reflecting, and stop taking responsibility, everything becomes harder.

And being pissed off becomes... honestly?

Pretty reasonable.

This is why we can't have nice things.

# CHAPTER 3 - Politics and Incompetence

Politics is the only industry where you can be publicly terrible at your job, lie openly, contradict yourself, blame everyone else for your failures, accomplish nothing, get caught doing shady deals, misuse taxpayer money, embarrass the people you represent… and STILL get reelected - sometimes with a bigger margin than before.

If any other profession worked like politics, the world would collapse in a week.

Imagine if your mechanic functioned like Congress:
They promise to fix your car.
They break it more.
They blame the previous mechanic.
They charge you double.
They hold a press conference about the importance of transportation equity.
They start a re-election campaign.
They ask you for a donation.

That's politics.

And that's why this chapter exists - because the political world is full of clowns… just wearing different makeup.

# Both Sides Are Full of Clowns - Just Different Makeup

People love to pretend their side has moral superiority and the other side is a collection of unhinged maniacs.

The truth?

They're ALL unhinged maniacs.

The only difference is branding.

One side paints their clown makeup with patriotic colors and cries about tradition.

The other paints theirs in earth tones and cries about progress and vibes.

But underneath the face paint, politicians on BOTH sides:
lie constantly,
blame each other for everything,
peddle fear like it's going out of style,
raise money off every problem,
pretend to be heroes,
pretend the other side is the devil,
accomplish absolutely nothing.

It's not a political system.

It's a circus.
A bipartisan circus.

A bipartisan circus stocked with:
rodeo clowns,
stunt clowns,

birthday clowns,
terrifying sewer clowns,
and elite, high-budget corporate clowns.

Every few years, Americans gather around to choose which clown gets to hold the flaming baton next.

This is why we can't have nice things.

## The Senator Who Said Nothing... Beautifully

I once watched a senator talk for 12 full minutes.

Twelve.

He answered a question with such confidence, such poise, such rhetorical polish…

…and didn't say one actual thing.

Not one.

It was like listening to someone read a fortune cookie inside a motivational poster inside a horoscope.

He said things like:

"We must continue to prioritize the priorities that Americans prioritize."

Sir…

That means ABSOLUTELY NOTHING.

Yet people watching nodded like he'd delivered the Sermon on the Mount.

This is the political trick:
speak confidently while saying nothing.

## Politicians Who Say Everything Except What Matters

Politicians have a supernatural ability to talk endlessly while avoiding the actual question like it's radioactive.

Ask:

"Do you support this bill?"

They respond with:

"I support the American people and believe in our nation's future."

Translation:
No.
Or maybe yes.
Or maybe they have no idea.
But they're not saying it.

Ask:

"Where did the money go?"

You'll hear:

"We're exploring budgetary pathways that strengthen fiscal transparency moving forward."

Translation:
We lost it.
Or spent it.
Or gave it to our donor's nephew.
But we'll never admit it.

Ask:

"Why haven't you fixed the problem you campaigned on?"

They'll say:

"We're actively forming a committee to better understand the ongoing situation."

Translation:
We have no intention of doing that.

Politicians speak in an ancient dialect known as Ambiguity Salad - a mixture of buzzwords, recycled slogans, vague assurances, and phrases stolen from corporate onboarding manuals.

It sounds meaningful.

It means nothing.

## How Broken Systems Stay Broken - On Purpose

People love saying, "The system is broken!"

No.
It isn't.

The system is working perfectly - for the people who designed it.

Broken systems:
generate outrage,
encourage loyalty,
divide voters,
create endless campaign topics,
motivate donations,
provide talking points,
ensure job security.

If politicians fixed:
healthcare,
cost of living,
taxes,
infrastructure,
education,
immigration,
housing affordability...

...they'd lose their greatest weapon: problems.

Problems are profitable.
Solutions are boring.

Broken systems are how politicians manipulate the public into thinking they're essential.

If they ACTUALLY fixed things, we might realize we don't need half of them.

# The City Council and the Fallen Stop Sign

A stop sign fell over in my old neighborhood.

Just fell.

Simple fix: 10 minutes, $48, one worker.

It took the city six months to fix it.

During those six months:
three subcommittees were formed,
four meetings were held,
two "community impact listening sessions" occurred,
a neighborhood poll was conducted,
the vote was postponed twice,
the budget was "reviewed,"
the study was "studied,"
and the sign continued lying on the ground like a drunk Frisbee.

Finally, a city worker installed a new sign.

It took him TEN MINUTES.

This wasn't incompetence.

This was bureaucracy functioning EXACTLY as intended:
slow,
expensive,
inefficient,
committee-driven,
allergic to efficiency,
and totally disconnected from citizens.

If aliens landed tomorrow, studied our government, and left, they'd report:

"Humans have no idea how to accomplish basic tasks."

This is why we can't have nice things.

# The Political Pendulum: Outrage → Promises → Disappointment → Repeat

Every election cycle is emotional Groundhog Day.

**STEP 1: Outrage**
People are furious.
They want change.
They want justice.
They want anyone BUT the current group of clowns.

**STEP 2: Promises**
Politicians start their speeches.
They promise:
"This time we'll fix everything!"
"We're fighting for YOU!"
"Your voices matter!"
"We are the change we seek!" (what does that even mean?)

It's all theatrical nonsense.

**STEP 3: Disappointment**
They get elected.
The public hopes.
The public waits.
Nothing happens.

Everyone slowly realizes:

"Oh… they're just like the last ones."

**STEP 4: Repeat**
A new election arrives.
People get mad again.
Everyone says:

"This time it's different!"

No.
It isn't.
And it won't be.

The political pendulum swings back and forth like a screen door in a hurricane - but the view never changes.

## Everything Is a Culture War Until We Need Roads

Politics today is basically one long, exhausting culture war.

Not a war over solutions.
Not a war over real issues.
Not a war over policy.

A war over nonsense.

People scream at each other online like rabid ferrets fighting over a french fry (or is it a freedom fry) - and nine times out of ten, the thing they're fighting about barely affects anyone's daily life.

Everything becomes a culture war:
books,
electronics,
logos,
phrases,
commercials,
packaging,
bathrooms,
colors,
cereal,

movies,
cartoon characters,
plastic straws,
holiday cups,
mascots,
phrases taken out of context,
tweets from 2011.

It all becomes "the downfall of America."

But then something real happens.

A bridge collapses.
A water main bursts.
A road caves in.
A wildfire starts.
A sewage line explodes.
A power grid fails.

Suddenly EVERYONE gets very quiet.

The people screaming about culture wars start yelling:

"WHY ISN'T THIS FIXED?!"

The truth?

It's not fixed because politicians were too busy arguing about cartoon characters.

## The Bridge Collapse That United Everyone for 18 Minutes

A bridge collapsed last year.

Major road.
Major damage.

For ONE GLORIOUS MOMENT - about 18 minutes - the entire political spectrum united under one shared belief:

"This is bullshit."

Nobody argued.

Nobody debated.

Nobody cared who voted for whom.

Everyone was just shocked the bridge wasn't maintained.

But around minute 19?

The culture war rebooted.

Someone tweeted something dumb.
Politicians blamed each other.
News hosts took sides.
Pundits spun narratives.
Social media melted down.

But for 18 minutes?

Peace.
Unity.
Focus.

Real-life consequences make politics simple again:

Fix the damn bridge.

# Everyone Is a Culture Warrior Until Reality Hands Out Consequences

Politicians LOVE culture wars because they require:
no money,
no planning,
no competence,
no cooperation,
no accountability,
no results,
and maximum attention.

Outrage is cheap.
Infrastructure is expensive.

Internet fights are free.
Water systems cost billions.

Culture wars win votes.
Road repairs don't.

A politician will spend six months screaming about a cartoon rabbit being "too sexy now"…

…but ask them to fix a collapsing highway?

"Oh wow, uh, that's complicated, we need studies, committees, long-term frameworks…"

Just pour the asphalt, man.

# The Mayor's "Listening Tour" Instead of Fixing Potholes

A mayor in a nearby town announced a "listening tour" because potholes were out of control.

Instead of fixing the potholes, he:
scheduled 14 community meetings,
held press conferences,
made posts about "engagement,"
took photos with distressed citizens,
wore a reflective vest for optics.

One woman asked him directly:

"Why don't you just fix the potholes?"

He said:

"We're developing a long-term listening-centered approach."

Sir…

The asphalt is RIGHT THERE.

Just put it in the hole.

This is why we can't have nice things.

# When Real Problems Hit, Politics Disappears Instantly

You want to see how fake political division really is?

Wait for a disaster.

A blizzard hits - suddenly everyone is on the same team.
A wildfire starts - suddenly nobody cares about slogans.
The lights go out - suddenly everyone wants government help.
A water pipe bursts - suddenly Twitter activists become plumbers' biggest fans.

You know what nobody has ever said during a crisis?

"Before you rescue me, I need to know your political stance."

No.

Everyone says:

"Help."

Reality is the great equalizer.
Culture wars disappear when consequences arrive.

## The Water Main Geyser That Ended Facebook Politics for 3 Hours

A water main broke in my old neighborhood.

A literal geyser blasting out of the sidewalk.

Before the break, our neighborhood Facebook group was a nonstop political battleground:
insults,
memes,
conspiracy theories,
long, emotional rants,

people arguing about recycling bins.

Then the water shut off.

Instantly everyone posted the SAME thing:
"Does anyone know when the water is coming back on?"
"Does the city know?"
"Who do we call?"
"This is ridiculous!"

Not one person blamed liberals.
Not one person blamed conservatives.
Nobody argued about ideology.
Nobody mentioned culture wars.

They united under one shared emotion:

Annoyance.

And then, as soon as the water was fixed, everyone went back to political cage fighting.

## Culture Wars Are Dessert. Infrastructure Is Vegetables.

Culture war issues:
are emotional,
divide people,
get attention,
are cheap,
involve slogans,
are symbolic,
require no work,
result in zero actual change.

Infrastructure:
affects EVERYONE,
requires real planning,
costs money,
takes time,
forces cooperation,
involves accountability,
has life-or-death consequences.

Politicians prefer dessert.
People NEED vegetables.

But we keep electing people who'll serve us a cake made of outrage and empty promises.

Then, when reality hits, we all realize:

"Wait - where's the nutrition?"

## Why Politics Always Feels Like a Circus

It's a circus because:
there are ringmasters,
there are acrobats,
there are jugglers,
there are tightrope walkers barely hanging on,
and there are clowns,
so many clowns,
endless clowns,
clowns upon clowns,
clowns running the clown factory.

We don't have leaders.
We have performers.

We don't have governance.
We have theatrics.

We don't have priorities.
We have talking points.

We don't have results.
We have fundraising targets.

It's exhausting.
It's predictable.
It's maddening.

And that's why everyone in this country is at least a little pissed off.

## Why This Chapter Matters

Politics may not be the ONLY broken system in America - but it's the one that breaks everything else.

When leadership is:
incompetent,
distracted,
unserious,
focused on winning, not governing,
addicted to culture wars,
allergic to responsibility,
unwilling to fix anything…

…then EVERYTHING gets harder.

Traffic gets worse.
Housing gets worse.
Healthcare gets worse.
Infrastructure decays.

Costs rise.
Public frustration increases.

And daily life becomes a never-ending series of stupid obstacles.

Things don't fall apart because society is doomed.
They fall apart because our systems are maintained by people who care more about Twitter trends than sewer lines.

And THAT is why politics is one of the biggest sources of anger in modern life.

You're not crazy.
You're not overreacting.
You're not "too sensitive."

You're living in a country run by circus performers fighting over imaginary culture wars while ignoring the real world collapsing around them.

Of COURSE you're pissed off.

This is why we can't have nice things.

# CHAPTER 4 - Bureaucracy: The Art of Doing Nothing Slowly

There are few things in life more consistent than government bureaucracy:
Death,
Taxes,
And a line at the DMV that makes you question your will to live.

Bureaucracy is the only system on Earth that can take a simple idea, wrap it in unnecessary processes, assign it six case numbers, forward it to three wrong departments, lose it twice, "escalate" it to nobody, and finally tell you to "come back tomorrow," even though the person telling you that is the same person you spoke to yesterday - and they still haven't moved.

Government offices don't run on efficiency.

They run on something far more powerful:

Inertia.

Bureaucracy is the art of doing nothing, slowly, expensively, publicly, and with laminated signage.

And it doesn't matter which office you go to - DMV, SSA, city planning, county clerk, building permits, zoning, licensing, utilities - they all operate like their mission statement is:

"Making life harder than it needs to be since the beginning of time."

This is why we can't have nice things.

# Government Offices Thrive on Inefficiency

Some people believe government workplaces are inefficient because of underfunding, understaffing, or outdated systems.

Wrong.

Government offices are inefficient BY DESIGN because efficiency threatens the one thing bureaucracies value most:

Job security.

Think about it:
If things worked smoothly,
If the systems were updated,
If forms were simplified,
If people could get in and out without a panic attack,

…half the jobs in these buildings would become unnecessary.

Efficiency is the enemy.

Chaos is job protection.

If the DMV finished your renewal in 10 minutes instead of 3 hours, someone in the back office might have to actually work.

Imagine the horror.

Government inefficiency isn't an accident.

It's their version of sustainability - the only thing they deliberately sustain.

# Why Nobody in a Government Office Is Ever in a Hurry

You could take a nap in the waiting room at any government office, wake up, and see the same people moving at the same speed as if time were a suggestion.

Government workers operate in their own time zone:

Government Standard Time

Which is roughly:
One real minute = four bureaucracy minutes
One real hour = "We'll be with you shortly"
One real day = "Try again Monday"

The pace is glacial.

Actually, no - glaciers move faster.

Glaciers are out there carving valleys, reshaping continents, and fueling oceans.

Government workers are out there stapling papers at a pace a sloth would call "lethargic."

You ever notice nobody at a government office ever looks stressed?

Not rushed.
Not pressured.
Not motivated.
Not "Oh wow we should probably get through this crowd."

Just calmly vibing in their ergonomic chairs as the lobby fills with desperate souls who have been waiting so long they start discussing existential philosophy with strangers.

This isn't laziness.
This is institutional leisure.

A lifestyle.

## The Absurd Processes for Simple Tasks

Let's talk about the real fun:
simple tasks that somehow become complicated.

Want to change your address?

Better bring:
Two proofs of residency,
A piece of mail from 1998,
Your original birth certificate,
A notarized letter from your favorite childhood teacher,
A urine sample,
Three passport photos,
And possibly a sacrificial goat.

And even then the clerk will say:

"Oh, we can't process this today. Jeremy is on lunch."

Jeremy has been on lunch since Reagan was in office.

Need to renew your license?

That's a half-day expedition requiring:
An appointment that doesn't exist,

A form that only prints correctly in Internet Explorer,
A waiting room chair designed by medieval torturers,
A number ticket 40 digits higher than the current one,
A pen that doesn't write,
And a clerk who calls "B-17" when you're holding "B-16," but somehow insists they didn't.

When you finally make it to the counter, the clerk says:

"Actually, you're in the wrong line."

This is why we can't have nice things.

Need a building permit?

Oh boy.

Be prepared for:
A 28-page form,
Five signatures from people who don't work there anymore,
A map of your backyard drawn to scale,
A drought-impact statement,
A soil displacement analysis,
A parking plan,
A noise mitigation promise,
And a photocopy of your soul.

All of this… just to replace your fence.

Want a copy of a document they lost?

They always say:

"We don't lose things."

Then they immediately go into the back room for 25 minutes and come back empty-handed like they've just solved a murder.

## The Lady Who Needed a Signature

Once, I watched a woman try to get a SINGLE signature to approve her daycare license renewal.

One signature.
One pen stroke.
One second of effort.

It took three hours.

The clerk said:
The supervisor needed to sign it.

The supervisor said:
It had to go through intake first.

Intake said:
They didn't know what she was talking about.

Another clerk said:

"Oh, this is a different form."

The woman said:

"No, this is the form YOUR OFFICE gave me."

They responded:

"Hmm. Let me check with someone in the back."

They always check with "someone in the back."

I'm convinced "someone in the back" is a hamster.

Finally, the supervisor returned and said:

"Actually, we can't sign this until tomorrow."

Tomorrow?!

Why?

Did the pen need to rest?
Was it union-mandated?

The woman's soul left her body.
Mine did too.

This is why we can't have nice things.

## Real Examples of Pointless Red Tape

Let's take a tour through some real-life bureaucratic nightmares the average citizen endures:

**Needing an appointment to make an appointment**
Yes, this happens.
Certain offices will tell you:
"You can't make that appointment unless you have an appointment to make it."
This is the bureaucratic version of a snake eating its own tail.

**The "Signature Must Be Blue Ink Only" rule**
As if black ink causes systemic collapse.
You hand them the form and they stare at it like you forged a passport.

## The "We don't accept scanned documents, only faxed ones" rule

Fax machines died 15 years ago.
Only government buildings still cling to them like a nostalgia item.

## ID rules that contradict themselves

"Your license isn't a valid ID."
"I need a valid ID to verify your identity before renewing your license."
"We can't verify your license without a valid ID."
This is basically a psychological trap.

## The 'We close at 4:30' office that stops taking people at 2:10

Shuts down early.
No consequences.
No shame.

## The automated phone system that actively tries to ruin your day

"Press 1 for more options."
"Press 2 to hear these options again."
"Press 3 to return to the previous menu."
"Press 4 to scream into the void."
"Press 5 to be disconnected."

## The system that requires you to mail in a form… to ask permission to mail in another form

Somewhere, a bureaucrat is smiling.

## A document needing three signatures - each from an office 45 minutes apart

By the time you get the signatures, the first one has already expired.

**The office that still uses Windows XP and tells you the system is down**
OF COURSE it's down.
XP wasn't designed to run past 2005.

**The worker who insists you filled something out wrong... but refuses to tell you how**
They just circle it and push it back like a disappointed teacher.
"This isn't correct."
"Okay... what's wrong?"
"It's just not correct."

This is why we can't have nice things.

## Why Bureaucracy Exists (and Will Never Go Away)

Bureaucracy is profitable - not financially, but politically.

It creates:
departments,
jobs,
funding,
committees,
appropriations,
budgets,
reportable metrics,
internal promotion opportunities.

Bureaucracy is a self-replicating organism.

It creates problems only it can solve, then pretends it's the hero for solving them.

And every year, the organism grows:

more rules,
more forms,
more offices,
more staff,
more red tape,
more nonsense.

If the government simplified everything tomorrow, millions of positions would become unnecessary.

So instead, they complicate things to justify existing.

## It's Not the Front-Line Workers - It's the System

Before we go any further, let's make something very clear:

The line-level government employee is not the problem.

They're not sitting behind that counter dreaming up new ways to ruin your day.
They're not personally responsible for the seven forms, the contradictory rules, the ink color requirements, or the labyrinth of pointless steps you're forced to navigate.

They're just trying to survive.

Most of them are:
underpaid,
overworked,
understaffed,
underappreciated,
and doing the best they can in a system built entirely out of red tape and printer errors.

They're following rules they didn't write, procedures they don't understand, and policies created during the Nixon administration by some long-retired bureaucrat who thought paperwork was a personality.

You can tell who the front-line workers are by their eyes.

They all have the same look - a sort of existential glaze that says:

"I don't make the rules. I just survive them."

These people aren't trying to slow you down.

They're trying to avoid getting written up because they dared to exercise common sense in a workplace where common sense is considered "wildly unauthorized decision-making."

## The Real Culprits: The Bureaucrats Above Them

The ones to blame are the mid-to-upper-tier bureaucrats - the individuals who:
sit in meetings all day,
draft new rules to justify their job titles,
never actually interact with the public,
create policies so confusing even THEY don't understand them.

These are the folks who decide:
what forms exist,
how many signatures they need,
what ink color is acceptable,
what documents are required,
which outdated technologies must still be used (fax machines forever!),
and what arbitrary nonsense everyone must follow.

They're the ones who turned simple tasks into obstacle courses.

And they do it for the same reason government inefficiency thrives:

Fear of getting sued in a hyper-litigious society.

Bureaucracy's favorite phrase is:

"We need to protect ourselves legally."

Which is bureaucratic code for:

"Someone sued us 18 years ago, so now everyone must suffer forever."

Somewhere, someone once:
filled out a form wrong,
claimed they "weren't informed,"
filed a lawsuit,
and won $2,500 in a settlement.

That one lawsuit from 2006 is now the origin story of why:
you need four proofs of residency,
a notarized letter,
a signed affidavit,
two witness statements,
and three forms of ID to update your address.

This is why we can't have nice things.

## The System Is Designed to Avoid Risk - Not Help People

Government systems aren't built to help citizens.

They're built to avoid:

lawsuits,
liability,
responsibility,
blame,
accountability.

That's why rules get more complex every year.

That's why offices cling to outdated processes.

That's why nothing can be simplified.

Simplifying anything increases the risk that something might go wrong - and bureaucrats fear risk like cats fear cucumbers.

So instead of improving systems, they add:
more forms,
more signatures,
more steps,
more deadlines,
more restrictions,
more disclaimers.

If they could, they'd add a form to apologize for the confusion created by their other forms.

Actually, scratch that - they HAVE.
It's Form D-22: "Acknowledgment of Improper Acknowledgment."

This is why we can't have nice things.

## The Front-Line Employees Are Hostages Too

The person behind the glass window?

They're not your enemy.

They're another victim.

They're stuck in a job where:
they can get reprimanded for using the wrong stapler,
their supervisor quotes rules from a binder last updated in 1994,
they need approval to approve someone else's approval,
they get yelled at daily for things they didn't control,
they must enforce rules they think are ridiculous,
they cannot use common sense without getting in trouble.

They aren't the jailer.
They're the inmate who gets to hand out lunch trays.

If they bend a rule to help you?
They risk losing their job.

If they follow the rules strictly?
You think they're the villain.

They can't win.

They're trapped inside a machine built by people who haven't stood in a public-facing line since the Clinton administration.

So they play it safe.

They follow procedure.

They stamp the wrong box, apologize, then stamp it again.

They enforce rules they don't even believe in.

Because inside every government office is one universal truth:

"If it isn't written down, approved, stamped, cross-stamped, initialed, and entered into the system twice, it might as well not exist."

This is why we can't have nice things.

## A Step-by-Step Guide to Filling Out a Completely Useless Form

Every government form is written like it was translated into English from English.

Here is a realistic guide:

**Step 1: Obtain Form X-17-B-Revised-Alpha-Draft-2021**
You will ask the front desk for the form.
They will give you Form X-17-C by accident.
You will wait 40 minutes to ask again.
They will act like you're asking for a nuclear launch code.

This is why we can't have nice things.

**Step 2: Fill out Section A (Personal Information)**
This includes:
your name,
address,
phone number,
emergency contact,
and your "City-Assigned Residential Sub-Zone Identifier," which nobody knows because the city made it up last week.

Good luck.

## Step 3: Fill out Section B (Your Mother's Maiden Name and Proof You Exist)

You must list:
your mother's maiden name,
two references,
and your first pet's genealogy.

Along with three forms of identification including:
a state ID,
a passport,
and a photo of you holding today's newspaper for "verification."

## Step 4: Don't Sign Section C (Unless Specified to Sign Section C)

This rule will contradict itself twice on the next page.

## Step 5: Attach Supporting Documents

Required materials:
a bank statement,
a utility bill,
a holographic unicorn sticker,
a piece of mail you didn't open,
proof of residency,
and proof of proof of residency.

## Step 6: Submit Your Form

You hand it to the clerk.
They immediately tell you:

"You filled out the old version."

There is always a new version.
It is never publicly available.

**Step 7: Start Over**
Cry a little.
Begin again.

**Step 8: Wait for Approval**
Processing time:

"6 - 9 weeks unless delayed, extended, replaced, or otherwise impacted by system migration."

System migration = they unplugged something.

**Step 9: Receive a Letter Saying You Did Something Wrong**
The letter is written in bureaucratic riddles:

"Your application was incomplete due to incompletion."

You call for clarification.
They tell you:

"Come in person."

**Step 10: Return in Person**
The clerk looks at your form and says:

"Oh, we could have fixed this over the phone."

This is why we can't have nice things.

## Why This Chapter Matters

Bureaucracy is one of the purest sources of modern frustration.

It is the perfect combination of:
incompetence,

confusion,
inefficiency,
arrogance,
outdated systems,
pointless rules,
and relentless slowness.

It embodies everything this book is about - everyday nonsense that makes reasonable people angry.

No matter how patient, calm, kind, or resilient you are, a few hours in a government building will transform you into someone who contemplates citizenship in a new country.

And the punchline?

Every future chapter - cheaters, bad parents, entitled people, corporate nonsense, scammers - they all intersect with bureaucracy eventually.

Government inefficiency isn't just annoying.

It is the backdrop of modern life.

And every time we try to get something done…

they find a new way to make it harder.

This is why we can't have nice things.

# CHAPTER 5 - Economics and Inequality

Let's talk about money - specifically, the fact that nobody has any.

Or more accurately, everyone has money for about nine minutes after payday, and then it evaporates like someone sprinkled it into a bonfire.

Meanwhile, the cost of everything keeps climbing toward the stratosphere like it's trying to escape Earth's gravity.

We live in an economy where:
you work more,
you make less,
everything costs more,
companies give you less,
and somehow you're still told you "just need to budget better."

Budget better?

Buddy, I could track every penny with FBI-level precision and it still wouldn't explain why eggs cost as much as a down payment.

This is the modern economy.

A giant hamster wheel where no matter how hard you run, someone keeps increasing the incline.

This is why we can't have nice things.

# Why Wages Don't Match the Cost of Living

Let's start with the biggest scam of all: wages.

Wages have barely moved in decades.
Cost of living has exploded into a financial supernova.

If wages and living costs were in a boxing match, cost of living would be Mike Tyson and wages would be a middle-school kid wearing floaties and crying.

In the last 40 years:
Housing prices have ascended to Mount Olympus,
Rent went from "affordable" to "who do I have to fight?,"
Groceries doubled, then doubled again,
Healthcare is now financially indistinguishable from extortion,
Utilities are inching toward luxury status,
Cars are priced like small mansions,
Insurance premiums rival mortgage payments,
Childcare requires selling a vital organ.

Meanwhile, wages barely budge.

Most companies treat raises like they're handing out limbs.

"We're proud to offer you a 2% increase this year."

TWO PERCENT?

At this point, 2% is an insult.
2% won't buy a loaf of bread.

And companies pretend they're being generous:
"We value our employees."
"We appreciate your hard work."

"We're committed to competitive pay."

Competitive with WHAT?

Medieval serfdom?

Meanwhile, executives get:
bonuses the size of small nations,
stock packages,
private jets,
personal drivers,
catered lunches,
offshore accounts,
vacation homes,
an extra vacation home for their dog.

And employees get:
a pizza party,
a lanyard,
an "Employee of the Month" certificate printed on the cheapest possible paper.

This is why we can't have nice things.

## How Corporations Invent New Ways to Nickel-and-Dime You

Corporations used to rip you off the old-fashioned way: charging more.

Now they've evolved into beautifully creative thieves.

They nickel-and-dime you with:
subscriptions,
fees,

add-ons,
upcharges,
downsizing,
shrinkflation,
"convenience" charges,
"processing" fees,
"activation" fees,
"maintenance" fees,
mandatory tipping prompts,
forced upgrades,
digital purchases,
app-exclusive charges.

The economy is one giant financial pickpocket.

Let's go through their greatest hits.

## 1. Subscriptions for Everything

Want to use your car's heated seats?
Subscription.

Want your TV to do basic features?
Subscription.

Want your phone's cloud storage?
Subscription.

Want your refrigerator to connect to Wi-Fi?
Subscription.

Soon water fountains will have:

"Subscribe for unlimited drinking."

## 2. Shrinkflation

This is where products get smaller but the price stays the same, and companies gaslight you about it like YOU'RE the crazy one.

"Didn't this bag used to be full?"
"No, it's ALWAYS been 6 chips."

Right.

The people designing packaging for chips are evil geniuses.

They fill the bag 90% with air and 10% with three broken chips and a crumb.

Cereal boxes?

You open the box, look inside, and wonder if someone stole half your breakfast.

Toilet paper rolls?

They used to be thick and plush.
Now you can see through them like a piece of tracing paper.

This is why we can't have nice things.

## 3. Fees for Things That Don't Require Fees

Want to buy tickets online? Fee.
Want to load money onto a card? Fee.
Want to pay your bill online? Fee.
Want to use self-checkout? Fee.

SELF-checkout.

You're doing THEIR job and paying THEM for the privilege.

What's next?

Breathing fee?
Standing fee?
Thinking-about-it fee?

## 4. Tipping Prompts for Everything
We've entered a new era: guilt-tipping.

Every touch screen in America demands a tip:
for handing you a muffin,
handing you a bottle of water,
printing a receipt,
making eye contact,
flipping a screen toward you.

I once bought a pack of gum and the screen asked:

"How much would you like to tip?"

FOR WHAT?!

The gum didn't even scan itself.

## 5. Airline Fees That Feel Like Extortion
Airlines charge for:
seats,
picking seats,
sitting too close to seats,
luggage,
carry-ons,
oxygen circulation,
"comfort,"
water,
snacks,
boarding early,

boarding late,
existing.

At some point they'll charge:

"Bathroom access: $12.99"

This is why we can't have nice things.

## The Gig Economy Scam

The gig economy was marketed as:

"Freedom! Flexibility! Be your own boss!"

In reality:

"You now work for a trillion-dollar corporation with no benefits, no protections, and all the costs."

You're an "independent contractor" - basically a full-time employee without:
health insurance,
retirement,
PTO,
sick leave,
job security,
legal rights,
guaranteed wages.

But with:
wear and tear on your car,
gas expenses,
your own insurance,
out-of-pocket repairs,

self-employment taxes,
algorithmic punishments.

It's like being in a relationship where the other person:
uses your house,
your car,
your money,
your time,
your emotional labor,

...and then says:

"What we have is casual."

## The $0.47 Delivery

A driver once posted a screenshot showing:
6 miles,
22 minutes,
$0.47 payout.

Forty-seven cents.

I've found more money under couch cushions.

Support told them:

"Our dynamic pay algorithm determines fairness."

Your algorithm determines CRIME.

This is why we can't have nice things.

# Inflation Math That Makes No Sense

Inflation is the country's favorite gaslighting technique.

Economists say:

"Inflation is cooling."

But prices don't go down.
They just rise slower.

Imagine saying:

"The fire is slowing."

While your house still burns.

That's inflation.

You're told:
"supply chain issues,"
"labor shortages,"
"global pressures,"
"currency fluctuations."

But then record corporate profits get announced and suddenly:
no one mentions supply chains,
no one mentions shortages,
no one mentions fluctuations.

Funny how that works.

Corporate Inflation Logic:
Raise prices due to external factors.
External factors improve.

Keep prices high "for stability."
Give shareholders record dividends.
Consumers ask: "Will prices return to normal?"
Answer: "No :)"

This is why we can't have nice things.

## Why Working More Feels Like Getting Less

The people who came before us:
bought homes early,
had savings,
had retirement,
raised families on one income,
retired at 60.

Today:
two-income households still struggle,
full-time jobs barely cover basics,
side hustles supplement side hustles,
vacations feel fictional,
retirement seems mythical,
the only people buying homes are investors and lottery winners.

We work more than any industrialized nation.
We get less in return.

People today work:
50 hours,
60 hours,
70 hours,
overtime,
weekends,
holidays.

And still feel financially underwater.

## The Three-Job Worker Who Still Couldn't Afford Rent

I knew someone working:
retail full-time,
restaurant part-time,
Gig delivery on weekends.

SEVEN days a week.

Then their landlord raised rent $350 "due to market value."

Market value for WHAT?

Human despair?

They had a panic attack in the grocery store staring at strawberries.

This is why we can't have nice things.

## The American Dream: Now Available Only as a Souvenir

The American Dream now feels like:
a rumor,
a myth,
a collectible item you find on eBay.

Instead of:
home ownership,
stability,
upward mobility,

retirement.

Most people get:
rising rent,
rising debt,
rising bills,
rising costs,
rising stress.

And the economy keeps saying:

"Bootstraps."

What bootstraps?

People are barefoot out here.

## Top 15 Signs the Economy Is Actively Screwing You

Can't afford gas to get to your job.
Groceries cost more than old rent.
Paycheck evaporates instantly.
Rent spikes for no reason.
Financing groceries.
"Convenience fees" for inconveniences.
Tip screens everywhere.
Companies profit while you starve.
Homeownership = boss fight.
Insurance robbery.
$90 = one grocery bag.
All subscriptions renew the same day.
Responsibilities up, pay down.
Side hustle for your side hustle.
One flat tire = financial apocalypse.

This is why we can't have nice things.

## The Psychological Cost of Economic Inequality

The economy isn't just draining wallets - it's draining mental health.

People feel:
exhausted,
anxious,
hopeless,
furious,
defeated,
ashamed,
overwhelmed.

They blame themselves:
"Maybe I'm bad with money."
"Maybe I didn't work hard enough."
"Maybe I should've chosen a different career."

But the truth?

It's not you - it's the system.

A system designed by people who never struggle.
A system where wealth creates wealth and poverty creates obstacles.
A system where the average worker is fighting uphill while corporations ski downhill.

This is why we can't have nice things.

# Why This Chapter Matters

Economic frustration is the heartbeat of modern anger.

You can't understand:
political outrage,
social tension,
burnout,
resentment,
frustration,
cynicism,
and the daily irritations of life...

...without understanding the economics behind it.

People aren't angry for no reason.
People aren't stressed because of "poor budgeting."
People aren't working three jobs because they "love the grind."

They're doing it because the system demands more and gives less.

You're not greedy.
You're not lazy.
You're not unreasonable.

You're surviving an economic gauntlet designed by people who will never run it.

And THAT is why you're pissed off.

This is why we can't have nice things.

# CHAPTER 6 - Healthcare: Where Hope Goes to Die

If you ever want to experience true despair - not mild frustration, not "the Wi-Fi dropped during a Netflix finale" irritation - I mean the deep, soul-wilting kind that makes you question why humans formed societies at all - try navigating the American healthcare system.

Healthcare in America is not about health.

It's not about healing.

It's definitely not about compassion.

It is about:
billing,
coding,
insurance loopholes,
denials,
pre-authorization,
waiting rooms,
networks,
out-of-network fees,
and a bureaucratic maze so convoluted it could break the will of a Navy SEAL.

You can do everything "right" - pay premiums, stay insured, follow rules, pick in-network providers - and STILL end up financially destroyed for the crime of needing medical care.

Hope doesn't just die in the American healthcare system.

It takes a number, sits in a waiting room, fills out a clipboard, gets denied, and then dies.

This is why we can't have nice things.

## Cost vs. Care: The Great American Paradox

The U.S. somehow created a system that perfectly combines the highest medical costs in the world with the most confusing and inconsistent care ever conceived.

It's like paying $900 for a "luxury meal" and getting a microwaved burrito wrapped in contempt.

You could be:
bleeding,
broken,
feverish,
injured,
coughing up organs,
actively dying…

…and the first question you'll hear at intake is:

"Do you have insurance?"

Imagine if firefighters said:

"Your house is on fire? Great. Who's your provider?"

Or if police said:

"We'll stop the mugger as soon as we confirm coverage."

Your condition matters less than your insurance card. And if you're unconscious? Don't worry - they'll still send a denial letter that says:

"This treatment was not medically necessary."

Not medically necessary? My body was shutting down!
But sure, let Kevin in the claims department decide what counts as "necessary."

This is why we can't have nice things.

## Health Insurance: Weaponized Confusion

Health insurance is the only product where you pay thousands of dollars to a company whose business model is not giving you anything in return.

Their tools of the trade:
loopholes,
denials,
circular logic,
contradictory rules,
and forms written in dialects no living human speaks.

They use words like:
deductibles,
co-insurance,
formularies,
tiered networks,
facility fees,
pre-authorization.

None of it is intuitive.
Rocket science is intuitive compared to health insurance.

# Emergency Surgery, Denied

A woman needed emergency gallbladder surgery.

Insurance later sent a letter:

"Denied. Prior authorization required."

Prior authorization?
For an emergency?

What was she supposed to do?

"Hey BlueCross, I'm dying. Can I get approval real quick?"
Estimated wait time: 54 minutes.

This is why we can't have nice things.

# The Sorcery of Medical Billing

Medical billing is sorcery performed by stressed gremlins slapping random numbers into a spreadsheet.

You go in for a simple procedure and months later get:
a bill,
a revised bill,
another bill,
an Explanation Of Benefits ("This is NOT a bill," which always means "This is definitely a bill"),
a bill showing $0,
a collection notice.

You call and ask why.

The clerk responds:

"Oh, that's not a bill."

"But it says bill."

"Yes."

"And says payment due."

"Correct."

"So… it's a bill."

"No."

You hang up questioning not just the system, but reality itself.

## The Prices Border on Fantasy

Common charges include:
$6,000 ambulance ride,
$800 Band-Aid,
$3,200 Tylenol,
$78 facility fee,
$122 "miscellaneous supplies" (which I assume is dark magic).

## The $40 Gloves

One bill listed:

"Latex Gloves - $39.95"

What are they made of? Unicorn?
Dragon hide?
Ethically sourced moon leather?

This is why we can't have nice things.

## Waiting Rooms: Purgatory With Fluorescent Lighting

Every waiting room in America features:
chairs that cause scoliosis,
a dead plant,
a TV stuck on daytime talk shows,
coughing children,
someone arguing with paperwork,
someone talking on speakerphone,
someone called before you who CLEARLY arrived after you.

## The Man Who Ate a Full Meal

I once watched a guy eat:
a burger,
fries,
a burrito,
chips,
a slice of cake,
and a soda.

He finished the entire thing…
and STILL wasn't called back.

Only American healthcare can turn a waiting room into a five-course dining experience.

## The Insurance Portal: Abandon Hope All Ye Who Log In

You log in to check a claim and get:
"Unexpected error."
"Your session has expired." (You logged in 11 seconds ago.)
"Feature unavailable."
"Try again later."

Insurance portals are digital escape rooms with no solution.

## Pharmaceutical Pricing: Highway Robbery With Better Branding

Drug prices make absolutely no sense anywhere except here.
$9 drug in Canada → $487 in the U.S.
$30 drug in Europe → $1,300 in the U.S.

And somehow pharmaceutical companies defend this with:
innovation,
research,
development,
buzzwords.

Translation:

"We want money."

## Insulin: The Biggest Scam

Inventor sells patent for $1 to keep it affordable.

Today:
$300 per vial.
People ration doses.
People die.

This is why we can't have nice things.

## Why This Chapter Matters

Healthcare is the perfect storm of:
greed,
bureaucracy,
confusion,
legal loopholes,
corporate indifference.

It punishes people for being sick and bankrupts families for being human.

If frustration had a headquarters, it would be a hospital billing department.

This is why we can't have nice things.

# CHAPTER 7 - Social Media Made Everyone Worse

There was a time - not long ago - when you could go full days without knowing what thousands of strangers thought about absolutely everything.

You didn't know:
your cousin's vaccine conspiracy,
your coworker's meltdown,
your neighbor's new identity as a "crypto philosopher,"
the guy from high school who only communicates through Jeep memes.

People had opinions.
They just kept them to themselves.

Then social media said:

"Let's build a permanent digital archive of everyone's worst impulses."

And humanity said:

"Sounds amazing."

The result is a society that's:
dumber,
angrier,
more insecure,
constantly outraged,
addicted to validation,
allergic to nuance,

and 300% more likely to argue about meaningless nonsense at 2 AM.

This is why we can't have nice things.

## The Dopamine Carnival

Social media is a digital casino where the slot machines are notifications.

Every:
like,
comment,
follow,
DM,
retweet,
"someone is typing…,"

…is a tiny dopamine pellet dropped into your brain like you're a lab rat with Wi-Fi.

Real accomplishments used to bring joy.

Now it's:
a fire emoji,
a stranger liking a photo of your dog,
a video hitting 300 views,
someone commenting "lol."

You're not happy.
You're chemically manipulated.

## People Are Addicted to Arguing

Before social media, to argue you had to:

be present,
look someone in the eye,
risk consequences.

Now people wake up like:

"Who can I emotionally destroy before breakfast?"

Someone posts:

"I like apples."

Replies:
"So you HATE oranges?"
"Imagine liking fruit like a sheep."
"This is what's wrong with America."
"Educate yourself."
"Unfollowed."

There is no nuance.
No curiosity.
Just people trying to validate their worldview by drowning out others.

## Echo Chambers: Algorithm-Generated Realities

Algorithms don't care about truth.

They care about:
engagement,
emotion,
outrage.

You click one video about:
crystals,

keto,
UFOs,
essential oils,
prepping,
astrology…

…and the algorithm builds an entire universe around it.

You're not interacting with a person anymore -
you're interacting with their algorithm.

This is why everyone online seems unhinged.

## Influencers: Famous for Absolutely Nothing

Influencers are crowned not by talent, but by algorithms.

They are famous for:
lip-syncing,
pointing at text boxes,
unseasoned chicken,
half-hearted dances,
whispering into the camera,
giving basic advice like it's divine revelation,
filming themselves buying things.

And many somehow earn more than:
nurses,
teachers,
EMTs,
firefighters,
anyone useful.

This is why we can't have nice things.

## Why Every App Ruins Itself

Every social media platform follows the seven-step death cycle:
Starts good,
Gets popular,
Adds ads,
Copies competitors,
Becomes unusable,
Lies about "enhancing experience,"
Everyone complains but stays.

This is the circle of life online.

## Oversharing: The New National Sport

Privacy used to be normal.
Now it's suspicious.

People share:
breakups,
medical diagnoses,
trauma,
cheating scandals,
financial crises.

Someone gets dumped and immediately goes Live:

"I don't normally share this, but…"

They share EVERYTHING.

## The Loneliness Paradox

Social media gives:
more followers,
more notifications,
more noise,

and fewer:
friends,
connections,
conversations,
real support.

People feel more alone than ever.

We weren't built for endless comparison.
We weren't built for infinite input.

But the algorithm doesn't care.

## Why This Chapter Matters

Social media didn't destroy humanity.
It just put every flaw on blast and monetized it.

It ruined:
conversation,
empathy,
patience,
comprehension,
attention spans,
civility,
boundaries.

It industrialized outrage.

It mass-produced insecurity.
It amplified stupidity.

And every "suggested post," every "new feature," every "algorithm tweak" only accelerates the decline.

This is why we can't have nice things.

# CHAPTER 8 - Technology Was Supposed to Help… and It Made Everything Worse

There was a time when people genuinely believed technology would make life easier.
Simpler.
Streamlined.
More intuitive.

We pictured a future where:
machines made chores effortless,
devices synced smoothly,
information was accessible,
communication was instant,
and everything "just worked."

Instead, we got:
constant software updates,
apps that break every other Thursday,
glitchy devices,
subscriptions for things that used to be free,
smart gadgets with the IQ of a grapefruit,
voice assistants with listening skills worse than a distracted toddler,
and refrigerators that demand firmware updates.

Technology didn't simplify life.
It complicated it in ways that defy reason.

This is why we can't have nice things.

# "Smart" Devices That Aren't Smart

Tech companies slap "smart" on everything now.

Smart speakers.
Smart lights.
Smart locks.
Smart thermostats.
Smart plugs.
Smart litter boxes.
Smart forks.

At this point "smart" just means "battery-powered and annoying."

Most "smart" devices are:
unstable,
glitchy,
overly dependent on Wi-Fi,
slow,
hard to set up,
impossible to troubleshoot,
and painfully stupid.

Their real job seems to be:
confusing you,
freezing at crucial moments,
disconnecting randomly,
and demanding updates every 20 minutes.

Let's break it down.

# Smart Fridges

A fridge has three jobs:
keep food cold,

stay functional,
don't start a philosophical debate.

Instead, smart fridges now come with:
full touchscreens,
shopping apps,
calendars,
cameras,
voice integrations,
weather reports,
streaming apps (WHY?),
and Wi-Fi so unstable it makes dial-up look reliable.

Your $4,000 "smart" fridge proudly flashes:
"Cannot connect to server."

Of course it can't.
It's a refrigerator, not a NASA satellite.

It'll warn you that your yogurt expires in three days, but the second the power flickers, it turns into an expensive pantry.

And when the screen dies or glitches?
Congrats - you now own a very fancy dumb box with a broken iPad glued to the front.

This is why we can't have nice things.

# Smart Locks

A normal lock works in:
rain,
sun,
snow,
darkness,

power outages,
nuclear winter.

Smart locks work ONLY when:
the Wi-Fi is stable,
your phone battery isn't dead,
the app isn't crashing,
the firmware is updated,
Mercury isn't in retrograde,
and the router gods approve.

Otherwise, you're standing on your porch explaining to your confused neighbor:

"My door needs a software update."

This is the future. Not flying cars. Not teleportation.
Waiting for your front door to download version 3.6.1.

This is why we can't have nice things.

---

## Smart Lights

Traditional lights:
Flip. On.

Smart lights:
Open app,
Wait,
Wait more,
App freezes,
Reopen,
Tap wrong room,
Fix it,
Error message,

Try again,
Finally turns on,
Somehow changes color by mistake.

Then at 2 a.m., they update themselves and your whole house flashes like you're being raided by SWAT. Even the dog looks around like, "What felony did you commit?"

## Smart TVs

Smart TVs freeze more than Windows 95.

You turn it on:
Black screen. Spinning wheel. Frozen menu. Wrong input.
Ad for a streaming service you don't have.
Update required.
Another update.
Crash.

Your TV is so busy trying to be a computer that it forgot how to be a television.

You hit the power button and it feels like the TV sighs:
"Whoa… slow down… I need a minute to process existing…"

This is why we can't have nice things.

## Updates That Break Things That Used to Work

One universal law of modern tech:

If it ain't broke, update it until it is.

Companies release updates more often than teenagers change moods. They swear these updates "improve stability," but every update makes the device less stable.

You update your phone and suddenly:
battery dies faster,
apps crash,
Bluetooth disappears,
photos corrupt,
keyboard lags,
widgets rearrange themselves like drunken Tetris blocks.

Update notes are always the same:
"Bug fixes."
"Performance improvements."
"Security enhancements."

Translation:
"We changed things. Something WILL break."

Your phone used to last all day.
After the update, it dies at 2 p.m. if you look at Instagram the wrong way.

Your computer used to run smoothly.
Now it moves like a sloth wading through molasses.

Nobody asked for new emojis.
We just wanted battery life that didn't collapse by lunch.

This is why we can't have nice things.

# Everything Becoming a Subscription

Corporate brainwave of the century:
One-time purchase = one payment.
Subscription = money forever.

So now everything is a subscription.

You pay monthly for:
streaming,
cloud storage,
apps,
car features,
GPS updates,
security systems,
filters,
smart appliances,
and your toothbrush's "premium brushing analytics."

Companies now charge to:
remote start your car,
unlock heated seats,
use "turbo mode" on your vacuum,
open your own garage.

What's next?
"PAY $0.99 TO HEAT THE OTHER SIDE OF YOUR BURRITO."

Soon your toilet will proudly announce:
"Upgrade to Premium Flush™ for just $1.49/month!"

Trying to cancel? Good luck.
You'll be interrogated like you're defecting from a cult.

"Are you sure?"
"Are you REALLY sure?"
"What if we give you one free month?"
"What if we cut the price?"
"What if we send someone to your house to beg?"

Just let me go.

This is why we can't have nice things.

## Voice Assistants That Don't Listen - Just Like Real People

Voice assistants were supposed to be futuristic helpers.

Instead, they're incompetent children with hearing problems.

You say:
"Alexa, turn off the bedroom light."
She hears:
"Playing Nickelback."

You say:
"Siri, call Mom."
She hears:
"Setting 11 random alarms."

You say:
"Hey Google, what's the weather?"
It hears:
"Here are recipes for goat stew."

But whisper the word fart from three rooms away and Alexa wakes up like she's been summoned.

They ignore:
every useful command,
every clear sentence,
every simple request.

But they're always ready to:
buy something,
mis-hear something,
or creepily chime in uninvited.

You're in the middle of a private conversation and suddenly:
"I'm sorry, I didn't quite catch that."

Catch WHAT?

Nobody was talking to you.

This is why we can't have nice things.

## The Smart Vacuum That Declared War

One guy described how his smart vacuum turned itself on at 3 a.m., escaped the living room, dragged a sock down the hallway like a trophy, wrapped itself in the curtains, and screeched error beeps until he was sure burglars had broken in.

If robots ever take over, they're going to be loud, confused, and permanently stuck under the couch.

## The Smart Home Meltdown

Another guy's entire smart home collapsed because the Wi-Fi went out.
Lights: offline

Locks: frozen
Thermostat: stuck at 84°
Sprinklers: activated themselves
Doorbell: reboot loop
Vacuum: screaming
Speakers: "I'm sorry, I'm having trouble with that."

He said:
"My entire house is controlled by a $40 router from 2014."

This is why we can't have nice things.

## The Oven That Needed an App

A man tried to preheat his oven.
It refused until he logged into the companion app.

"I can't cook dinner because my stove needs a software update."

Try explaining that to your grandparents.
They'd beat you with a wooden spoon for dishonoring the kitchen.

## Top 10 Things Smart Devices Think They're Too Good For

Staying connected to Wi-Fi longer than 12 minutes.
Updating when you choose.
Not updating when you don't choose.
Responding to voice commands.
Maintaining battery life.
Remembering your settings.
Working during storms.
Working in sunlight.
Working in general.

Doing the ONE job they were purchased for.

This is why we can't have nice things.

## Tech Support: Psychological Warfare

Tech support's main job is not to help you.
It's to crush your spirit.

You can explain your issue perfectly and they'll still ask:
"Have you tried restarting it?"

Yes.
I've restarted it so many times it thinks it's stuck in a reincarnation loop.

Next:
"Have you unplugged the router for 30 seconds?"

I could unplug it for 30 days and it wouldn't fix the fact your firmware was written by a sleep-deprived intern.

Every call ends the same:

You're tired, angry, and questioning every life choice that led you to this moment.

This is why we can't have nice things.

## The Internet of Things: A Web of Annoyance

Welcome to the Internet of Things - where nothing can function on its own anymore.

Your:
lights,
locks,
fridge,
oven,
vacuum,
thermostat,
cameras.

All require:
apps,
Wi-Fi,
passwords,
subscriptions,
cloud storage,
random updates.

Your toothbrush sends data to the cloud.
Your vacuum emails you.
Your doorbell records your front porch like it's a crime documentary.

Your whole house turned into a needy toddler.

This is why we can't have nice things.

## Top 12 Ways Technology Has Ruined Simple Tasks

**Setting an alarm**
Used to be: tap a button.
Now: "Siri didn't understand the request."

**Watching TV**
Used to be: power → channel.

Now: update → sign in → lookup password → sign in again → reset password → sign in → crash → update again → spend 30 minutes trying to remember which app has the show you want to watch.

**Driving**
Used to be: steering wheel.
Now: accept 12 pop-ups WHILE merging.

**Paying bills**
Used to be: write a check.
Now: solve CAPTCHA to prove you're not a robot.

**Opening your garage**
Used to be: remote.
Now: "Cannot connect to server."

**Checking out in stores**
Used to be: cashier.
Now: you vs broken scanner vs guilt-trip tipping screen.

**Answering your door**
Used to be: "Who is it?"
Now: blurry screenshot of a stranger's chin.

**Turning on lights**
Used to be: switch.
Now: "Device offline."

**Calling someone**
Used to be: dial.
Now: "Contact not synced across devices."

**Listening to music**
Used to be: press play.
Now: log in → ads → subscribe or else.

**Cooking**
Used to be: heat food.
Now: "Please update the companion app."

**Using ANYTHING after age 40**
Used to be: common sense.
Now: "Why is this blinking? Why is that beeping? Why is the dishwasher TALKING?"

This is why we can't have nice things.

## Why This Chapter Matters

Technology was marketed as the great liberator.

Instead, it became:
a distraction,
a frustration,
an obstacle,
a money pit,
a surveillance system,
a glitchy mess,
and a subscription trap.

It didn't make us smarter.
It made life more complicated.

So every time:
your phone updates overnight,
your apps stop working,
your fridge disconnects,
your voice assistant misunderstands you,
your smart home collapses because the router blinked .

Just remember:

This is why we can't have nice things.

# CHAPTER 9 - Corporations Doing Dumb Shit

Corporations have mastered many things:
mass production, global logistics, maximizing profits, squeezing every ounce of labor out of employees, building glass towers to worship themselves.

But their greatest skill?

Doing dumb shit at massive scale.

If stupidity were an Olympic sport, corporate America would sweep the podium.

Gold, silver, bronze - all handed to executives who got bonuses for creating the problems they were hired to fix.

Everything corporations do feels like it was designed by people who have never interacted with a regular human being.

And the higher you go up the ladder, the less oxygen seems to reach the brain.

This is why we can't have nice things.

## Pointless Rebranding: The Corporate Midlife Crisis

Rebranding is corporate Botox.

Cosmetic. Expensive. Unnecessary.
Solves absolutely nothing.

A company will be falling apart -
profits down, customer satisfaction in the toilet, staff quitting in waves -
and their bold strategic solution is:

"Let's round the logo and pick a new shade of blue."

That's it.
That's the plan.

## The Three Laws of Corporate Rebranding

**The new logo is always worse.**
Either it's so minimalist it looks unfinished or it resembles something a college freshman made in PowerPoint.

**It costs millions of dollars.**
Money that could've gone to raises, better products, or customer service.
But sure - new font.

**It changes absolutely nothing.**
Your internet still sucks.
Your package still arrives late.
Tech support is still useless.
But the logo? Oh, that thing is vibes.

This is why we can't have nice things.

# The Company That Rebranded and Immediately Collapsed

A real corporation once spent over $200 million on a rebrand.

The new logo looked like a sideways letter S that had melted.

Customers hated it.
Stock dropped.
Confusion spread.

Within six months, they quietly crawled back to the old logo.
Executives still took home "innovation" bonuses.

You can't make this up.

# Customer Service Run by Robots

We used to call a number and get a person.
Maybe they were bored or slow, but at least they were human.

Now you call and get:
a robot, powered by mediocre code, pretending to care.

You: "Representative."
Robot: "I'm sorry, I didn't understand that."

You: "REPRESENTATIVE."
Robot: "You can also visit our website!"

That's corporate for:
"We'd rather you go away."

Eventually, after yelling "representative" like you're performing an exorcism, you finally get put on hold behind 416 other broken souls.

This is why we can't have nice things.

## The Illusion of Support

Corporations measure success in:
call deflection,
tickets closed,
chats per hour.

Not actual resolution.
Not satisfaction.
Just volume.

That's why most support calls end with:
no answer,
no solution,
no explanation,
and no hope.

You hang up knowing less than when you dialed.

## AI Chatbots: Digital Hell Gremlins

Companies love chatbots because:
they're cheap,
always available,
and never unionize.

But they're about as useful as a paper umbrella in a hurricane.

You type:
"How do I cancel my subscription?"

Bot:
"Here's a link to our holiday gift guide!"

You:
"Cancel."

Bot:
"I didn't understand. Would you like a 10% coupon?"

No. I want freedom.

After walking through 12 pointless menus, the bot finally asks:
"Would you like to speak to a representative?"

You click yes.
Bot: "All representatives are currently unavailable."
Then the chat closes itself like it died of shame.

This is why we can't have nice things.

---

## Companies Pretending to Care (Corporate Virtue Signaling)

Nothing is more pathetic than corporations cosplaying as activists.

Every Pride Month:
banks, oil companies, defense contractors, fast-food chains, and airlines all slap rainbows on their logos like they marched at Stonewall.

Then July 1 hits:
Logos go back to normal.
So does their "values."

Corporations care about one thing:

money.

Every public "stance" is a marketing decision.

This is why we can't have nice things.

## Corporate Caring Greatest Hits

### Greenwashing
"Eco-friendly" brands that:
overpackage,
waste materials,
pollute water,
and run factories off coal.
Their sustainability mission statement was written by a PR intern with a succulent on her desk.

### Performative Activism
"We stand with [Cause We Googled This Morning]."
Meanwhile, the CEO is funding politicians actively opposing that cause.

### Diversity Theater
"We believe in representation."
Executive team?
Looks like a mayonnaise commercial.

This is why we can't have nice things.

## Middle Managers Inventing Problems to Justify Their Jobs

Middle managers are professional chaos generators.

They exist to:
hold meetings,
make PowerPoints,
invent problems,
micromanage,
and prevent anything from getting done efficiently.

They're the human version of a software update:

You didn't ask for them, they show up at the worst time, and they make everything slower.

## The Middle Manager Lifecycle

Find a minor inconvenience.
Inflate it into a "strategic concern."
Schedule meetings.
Solve nothing.
Add new rules.
Create busywork.
Demand reports no one reads.
Take credit for improvements that never happened.

### Top 10 Projects Middle Managers Use to Ruin Everything:
New protocols no one understands.
Mandatory weekly meetings.
Workflow software everyone hates.
Pointless policy changes.
Dress code updates.
"Efficiency" projects that slow everything down.
Approval chains with 12 signatures.
Multi-step processes for simple tasks.
Endless performance reviews.
"Team-building" events that destroy morale.

Every time something that used to take five minutes now takes 19 steps, a middle manager got bored.

## Corporate Buzzwords That Mean Absolutely Nothing

Corporate language is a landfill of meaningless noise.

**Top bullshit buzzwords:**
"Leveraging synergy"
"Driving value"
"Right-sizing the workforce"
"Enhancing the customer journey"
"Optimizing bandwidth"
"Deploying scalable solutions"
"Reimagining innovation"

Executives love saying:

"We need to align our strategic priorities to optimize scalable synergy."

Translation:

"I have no idea what I'm talking about, but my salary says I should."

This is why we can't have nice things.

## HR Theater & Fake Culture

HR is necessary.
But modern HR has drifted into performance art.

They don't primarily:

defend employees,
fix culture,
protect whistleblowers,
reduce burnout.

They do:
send newsletters,
schedule icebreakers,
assign mandatory online training,
enforce weird dress code rules,
hand out "Appreciation" cupcakes instead of raises.

HR exists to protect the company, not you.

This is why we can't have nice things.

## The HR Director Who Tried to Fix Morale With Cupcakes

One company had:
overworked staff,
bad pay,
high turnover,
toxic leadership.

HR's solution?

"Cupcake Friday."

Not more staff. Not better pay. Not fewer hours.
Cupcakes.

People still quit.

# Corporate "Innovation" Nobody Asked For

Corporations love innovation, as long as it:
costs money,
complicates everything,
and irritates customers.

So we get:
new apps,
new loyalty programs,
new ordering systems,
new packaging,
new layouts…

…none of which solve any actual problem customers have.

No one ever said:

"I want this website to be harder to navigate."

Yet here we are.

# The Software Upgrade That Broke Everything

A big company replaced its entire system with a "streamlined platform."

Within 48 hours:
orders disappeared,
accounts duplicated,
invoices broke,
customer data vanished,
employees panicked,

people cried in the bathroom.

Leadership:
"We consider this rollout a success."

Of course they did.
They don't have to use it.

## Annual Layoffs: A Coward's Tradition

Nothing screams "strong leadership" like firing hundreds of people right before the holidays.

Executives call it:
restructuring,
realigning,
right-sizing.

It's layoffs.
Just layoffs.

They always say:
"This was a difficult decision."

No, it wasn't. You did it over catered lunch.

## The Layoff List Email

One company accidentally CC'd all 1,200 employees on an email containing the list of everyone being laid off.

People were checking it like it was the Hunger Games.

Leadership blamed:

"A technical glitch."

Sure.

## Corporate Data Breaches & Security Dumbassery

Corporations store:
credit cards,
Social Security numbers,
private messages,
purchase histories,
browsing habits,
biometrics.

Their security?
Held together with duct tape and hope.

They get hacked.
Your info leaks.
Their response:

"We take your privacy very seriously."

If that were true, they wouldn't keep passwords in a file called:
PASSWORDS_FINAL_3.xlsx

This is why we can't have nice things.

## The Twelve Commandments of Corporate Stupidity

Thou shalt prioritize logos over functionality.

Thou shalt automate everything except what customers WANT automated.
Thou shalt blame the intern.
Thou shalt hold meetings that accomplish nothing.
Thou shalt innovate solutions for imaginary problems.
Thou shalt surveil employees while ignoring leadership failures.
Thou shalt send emails no one reads.
Thou shalt avoid responsibility at all costs.
Thou shalt misuse buzzwords with reckless abandon.
Thou shalt fire staff instead of fixing processes.
Thou shalt pretend to care about causes you do not care about.
Thou shalt always, ALWAYS forget that customers exist.

This is why we can't have nice things.

## Why This Chapter Matters

Corporations shape our daily lives - badly.

Every day they:
overcomplicate simple things,
prioritize profits over people,
design systems that don't work,
fake caring,
dodge accountability,
and consistently pick the dumbest possible option.

They aren't just greedy.
They're stupid.
And that stupidity touches everyone.

So every time a company:
rebrands pointlessly,
releases a broken update,
invents new rules,

weaponizes buzzwords,
"rightsizes" its workers,
or launches another chatbot that can't answer basic questions…

This is why we can't have nice things.

# CHAPTER 10 - Celebrities and the Cult of Forced Opinions

There was a time when celebrities stayed in their lane.

Actors acted.
Singers sang.
Athletes played sports.
Nobody cared what their stance was on monetary policy, vaccines, or geopolitical trade routes unless it involved DUIs, divorces, or drugs.

Fame used to be simple:
You performed.
People clapped.
You went home.

Now?

Being famous apparently comes with an honorary PhD in everything.

Political science? They've got opinions.
Economics? They've got think pieces.
Medicine? They've got "research."
Climate change? Hashtag activism.
Foreign policy? They watched one documentary and skimmed a thread.

We now live in an era where the guy who played Henchman #3 in *Rogue Velocity* believes he is fully qualified to lecture the nation on global agriculture policy.

It's madness.

This is why we can't have nice things.

## When Did Being Famous Become a PhD?

Somewhere along the way, we decided every celebrity must have a public position on every global event within 14 seconds of it happening.

Not just any position, either. It has to be:
bold,
passionate,
world-changing,
and posted as a Notes app screenshot on Instagram.

The media loves this.

A pop star posts, "We should do better," and suddenly:

BREAKING NEWS: POP STAR CALLS FOR GLOBAL REFORM

If a celebrity coughs, there's a panel segment.
If they blink slowly, Twitter decides it's "symbolic."

Meanwhile, real experts - the people who actually study this stuff for a living - are sitting there like:

"I literally wrote the textbook on this… but sure, let's quote the guy from the shampoo commercial."

Experts don't trend.
Experts don't go viral.
Experts don't sell ad space.

Celebrities do.

This is why we can't have nice things.

## The Rise of Performative Activism

Nothing captures celebrity activism better than the Great Instagram Black Square Era.

A complex, painful national moment…
summed up by millions of people posting a blank image and acting like they rebuilt society from scratch.

Celebrities led the charge:
black squares,
dramatic captions,
moody photoshoots in designer sweaters,
vague calls for "change" with no actual specifics.

The passion lasted about 48 hours.

Then the next trend hit -
iced coffee, a new Netflix show, whatever -
and the moral urgency evaporated.

That's celebrity activism in a nutshell:
temporary,
shallow,
aesthetic,
driven by optics.

Every week brings a new cause, new stance, new hashtag.
Celebrities rotate activism like outfits.

It's not conviction.

It's a calendar.

This is why we can't have nice things.

## The Celebrity Credibility Problem

Celebrities love giving advice in areas they have absolutely no business speaking on.

Actors selling wellness diets based on "energetic frequencies."

Singers endorsing detox teas that basically turn your insides into a slip-n-slide.

Models pushing jade eggs into places jade eggs should never go.

Influencers diagnosing mental illness using motivational quotes they found on Pinterest.

Then there are the TikTok pseudo-doctors - 20-year-olds with ring lights and zero credentials who believe they've discovered the truth about medicine because they watched three conspiracy videos and skimmed an abstract.

A glowy 22-year-old will stare into the camera and say:

"If you drink celery juice at sunrise, you can heal your trauma."

Oh good. Turns out we didn't need therapy, boundaries, or time. We just needed salad water.

It's like someone swapped real experts for a girl who usually films GRWM makeup videos and said, "Congratulations, you're a neurologist now."

This is why we can't have nice things.

## The Megaphone Problem

Celebrities have something experts don't:

A massive megaphone.

Millions of followers.
Instant visibility.
An audience ready to absorb whatever they say - even when it's complete nonsense.

One celebrity posts:

"The government is lying about food."

Suddenly 12 million people are convinced bananas are part of a mind-control program.

Another posts:

"Inflation is caused by negative energy and bad vibes."

And boom - there's a trending hashtag and a bunch of people who also failed high school economics reposting it like gospel.

People repeat celebrity opinions like scripture because they feel familiar.
They've seen them on screen, on stage, in interviews.

Familiar doesn't mean knowledgeable.
It just means loud.

This is why we can't have nice things.

# The Hypocrisy Olympics

Celebrities are world-class athletes in one event: hypocrisy.

They tell us to "eat clean and organic" while having private chefs, nutritionists, and food budgets bigger than our yearly income.

They preach public transportation while they hop on private jets to grab coffee in another time zone.

They urge us to "vote like your life depends on it" while living behind gates and guards completely insulated from the policies they're yelling about.

They post about minimalism and sustainability from a 27,000-square-foot mansion with a heated marble driveway.

And the all-time classic:

"We're all in this together."

Said from the balcony of a $40 million estate overlooking a city full of people who are definitively not "in this together" with them.

Nothing screams solidarity like a drone shot of your estate while you talk about sacrifice.

This is why we can't have nice things.

# The System That Created This Monster

To be fair, it's not just celebrities.

We built this circus.

The media needs content 24/7.
Real news takes effort. Celebrity nonsense is cheap and safe.
Fans demand constant commentary.

If a celebrity doesn't speak up, they're "complicit."

If they do speak up, they're "uninformed" or "performative."

There is no winning.

PR teams treat issues like branding opportunities.

"Is this stance morally important or trending?"
"Ideally both, but if we have to pick, go with trending."

Cancel culture demands a stance on everything.
Silence is punished.
Nuance is punished.
Being wrong is definitely punished.

So celebrities talk.

And talk.

And talk.

Not because they're experts.

Because the machine requires constant noise.

This is why we can't have nice things.

## Why We Keep Falling For It

We all know celebrities aren't experts.

But we still treat them like they are.

Why?

Familiarity feels like trust.

If you see someone's face enough, your brain decides you "know" them.

Parasocial relationships are powerful.
People feel like celebrities are part of their lives.

Celebrities do not feel the same way.

People want simple answers.

Experts say: "It's complicated."
Celebrities say: "Post this hashtag."

Guess which one gets more engagement.

Social proof is a drug.

If a million people like something, it feels true - even when it's absolute garbage.

This is why we can't have nice things.

## When Celebrities Actually Should Speak

Not all celebrity involvement is useless.

Some use their platform responsibly. The bar is just low.

It works when:

**They stick to their lane.**
Actors on acting, athletes on sports, musicians on the music industry? Great.
Henchman #3 from an action movie on geopolitical strategy? Hard pass.

**They use their money for actual good.**
Quietly funding schools, bail funds, hospitals, local projects - not just theatrical charity selfies.

**They admit they're not experts.**
One sentence could fix so much:
"I might be wrong."

**They stop pretending enlightenment came from a yoga retreat.**
You didn't become a philosopher because you did yoga on a cliff and drank a $17 green juice.

The celebrities who get this right do exist.
They're just drowned out by the ones live-streaming their enlightenment journey from a private jet.

This is why we can't have nice things.

# Why Celebrity Opinion Culture Pisses Me Off

Here's the core issue:

Celebrity opinion culture makes the world dumber.

It:
cheapens real activism,
spreads misinformation,

elevates fame over expertise,
drowns out people who actually know what they're talking about,
encourages fanbases to treat pop stars like political leaders.

We've built a world where:
singers are treated like economists,
actors like doctors,
influencers like therapists,
comedians like moral philosophers.

You wouldn't take dental advice from your barista.

You wouldn't ask your mechanic about nuclear treaties.

You wouldn't let your neighbor's cousin handle your brain surgery because he "does his own research."

So why in the hell are we asking celebrities for anything beyond entertainment?

This is why we can't have nice things.

## Why This Chapter Matters

Celebrities are great at what they do:
performing,
entertaining,
pretending,
singing,
dancing,
and being unreasonably attractive in good lighting.
But that does not make them qualified to guide civilization.
If I want advice, I'll take it from:
doctors,
scientists,

teachers,
researchers...

...people who actually studied the thing they're talking about.

Not someone whose main talent is memorizing lines written by someone else.

Fame isn't wisdom.
Followers aren't credentials.
Influence isn't intelligence.

And every time a celebrity:
gives medical advice,
posts a half-baked manifesto,
endorses conspiracy theories,
pushes dangerous diets,
or pretends they solved society while flying private...

This isn't just irritating - it's corrosive.

Because every time we elevate celebrity voices over real experts, the world gets a little dumber, a little louder, and a lot more confused. And when society keeps choosing charisma over competence?

This is why we can't have nice things.

# CHAPTER 11 - Why America Is Basically a Daily Headache

There are two kinds of headaches in life:
The kind caused by dehydration, stress, or terrible decisions.
The kind caused by living in America on a Tuesday.

And only one of those can be fixed with ibuprofen.

The modern American experience isn't one big crisis - it's a thousand tiny paper cuts delivered hourly. No single event triggers the rage. It's the accumulation. The layering. The slow drip of nonsense that turns a normal person into someone who mutters "unbelievable" sixteen times before lunch.

America doesn't assault you all at once.
It paces itself, like a petty marathon runner.

It wears you down like a river carving a canyon -
one infuriating drop at a time.

This is why we can't have nice things.

## America, the Group Project From Hell

If the country were a group project, it would work exactly like this:
One person is doing all the work.
One person won't stop making inspirational speeches.
One guy keeps asking, "Wait… what's this for again?"
One person insists the project is "rigged" and storms out.

And someone else shows up once every two weeks, contributes nothing, and still wants their name on the final slide.

Meanwhile, *you're* the one staying up until midnight trying to hold this circus together with duct tape and caffeine.

That's the American headache:
an endless group assignment where nobody reads the instructions.

## The Morning Everything Fell Apart

I recently lived a perfect illustration of this chapter.

All I needed - ALL I NEEDED - was to drop off a package at the post office.

Simple, right?

It should've been:
Walk in,
Hand box over,
Leave with dignity intact.

Instead, here's what actually happened:

I get to the post office and the line is already out the door. Good sign. A woman in front of me is arguing with the clerk because she wants to mail a cantaloupe. Not a box containing a cantaloupe. The literal fruit. The clerk keeps repeating, "Ma'am, produce needs special handling," and she keeps arguing like she's negotiating a hostage release.

Behind me, a man is loudly FaceTiming someone about his cat's medical procedure.

The self-serve machine is broken.

The pen is attached to the counter with a chain so short it's basically T-Rex-armed.

And when I *finally* get to the counter, the clerk says:

"You're in the wrong line."

THERE WERE NO LINES.
Just a cluster of lost souls drifting toward whatever fluorescent light felt warmest.

By the time I walked out, I had:
forgotten why I was there,
questioned the point of civilization,
aged seven emotional years.

And I realized - with complete clarity - that this feeling was not unique. This wasn't a moment - it was a diagnosis.

This is the American headache.
A thousand tiny frictions wrapped inside a "simple" task.

## The Daily Gauntlet of Mild Suffering

Every day in America feels like a low-budget obstacle course:
Your coffee order is wrong.
Your doctor's office makes you fill out 19 pages because you moved one street over.
Someone emails you "Per my last email…" like they're firing a warning shot.
The internet bill goes up for no reason other than "because we can."
A person in a giant SUV tries to merge using manifesting instead of turn signals.

None of these problems alone would ruin your day.
But together?

Together they become a full-blown migraine wearing sunglasses indoors.

The whole country operates on the principle of *cumulative irritation*.

Not enough to riot.
Just enough to fantasize about living in a cabin with no Wi-Fi.

## Everyone Is Annoyed, and Nobody Knows Why

Ask someone:
"Hey, how's it going?"

Nine out of ten Americans will respond with some variation of:
"I'm tired."

Not physically.
Not emotionally.
Existentially tired.

Tired in the soul.

Tired in a way eight hours of sleep cannot cure.

Because the American headache isn't about pain.
It's about drag - the exhausting mental friction of navigating systems that feel like they were designed by raccoons on energy drinks.

We're all constantly doing mental math:

"How bad is this going to be?"

"Is this worth the hassle?"
"Can I get out of this by dying?"

No wonder everyone walks around with the expression of someone who just stepped on a Lego.

## The Country Runs on Outdated Software (And It Shows)

Everything in America feels like it's operating on Windows 95 logic:
Healthcare is a maze with a boss fight.
Public systems haven't been updated since the Carter administration.
Customer service is basically performance art at this point.
Half of our infrastructure is held together with hope and zip ties.

It's not one thing that's broken.

It's everything, a little bit.

All at once.
All the time.
Forever.

No wonder we're pissed off.
No wonder we have headaches.
No wonder the national mood is one long sigh.

When a country is running ancient code, even simple tasks turn into loading screens.

This is why we can't have nice things.

# America: A Beautiful Disaster You Can't Quit

For all the chaos, the country has this bizarre charm.

Yes, the systems are terrible.
Yes, daily life feels like a test of emotional endurance.
But somehow - somehow - we keep going.

We keep trying.
We keep laughing.
We keep showing up at the post office even though it's a known trauma center.

The American headache isn't a sign we're broken.

It's a sign we're still participating.

Still hoping.
Still expecting things to make sense someday.
Still believing we deserve better.

That hope - even when it's delusional - is what keeps us from giving up completely.

# Why This Chapter Matters

The point of all this isn't:
"America bad."

It's:
"You're not crazy - daily life really IS harder than it needs to be."

You're not imagining the friction.
You're not overreacting to the nonsense.

You're not being dramatic when you stare into the void because your insurance app froze again.

You're experiencing what the rest of us are:

A country built on good intentions, duct tape, and processes nobody remembers creating.

America is basically one giant migraine with fireworks.

And if we don't laugh about it?

We'll end up screaming into the wind like the cantaloupe woman at the post office.

This is why we can't have nice things.

**PART II - DAILY LIFE: A COMEDY OF FRUSTRATIONS**
The everyday torture we all endure but rarely talk about without swearing.

# CHAPTER 12 - Neighbors: Proof That Hell Is Real

There are many indicators that hell is not a fiery cavern ruled by demons, but a modern suburb filled with humans who live close enough to ruin your life without meaning to.

People romanticize neighbors as "community," "support," or "togetherness."

Lies. All lies.

Neighbors are not support systems - they're random adults assigned to live within earshot of your sanity. Buying a home is basically gambling six figures on the hope that the person sharing a wall with you isn't a nocturnal furniture-dragger with unresolved emotional issues.

This is why we can't have nice things.

## The Loud Neighbor: America's Most Common Horror Villain

If you don't have loud neighbors, that means you are the loud neighbor.

Loud neighbors arrive in many forms:
The guy who treats Tuesday at 11 p.m. like Coachella pregame.
The woman who vacuums at midnight like she's punishing the carpet.
The couple who fights loudly, then has louder makeup sex like they're playing emotional ping-pong with your mental stability.

The TV watcher whose volume setting could broadcast to the International Space Station.
The family whose kids sprint upstairs like they're reenacting a medieval battlefield.

There's no in-between. It's either complete silence or a noise so mysterious you lie awake wondering:

What are they doing? Dropping refrigerators? Sacrificing appliances? Summoning spirits? Rehearsing for a competitive appliance-wrestling league?

It always happens at night - always. Loud neighbors don't believe in mornings. Their natural habitat is 1 a.m., when the rest of the world wants silence and they want to practice tap dancing in steel-toed boots.

This is how drywall becomes your spiritual test.

But noise isn't the only enemy, silence can be dangerous too.

This is why we can't have nice things.

## Petty Neighbors: The HOA Hall Monitors of Suburban Life

Petty neighbors are quieter but far more dangerous.
They don't attack with noise - they attack with rules.
They thrive on micro-aggressions, yard surveillance, and the intoxicating power of anonymous complaint hotlines.

These are the people who:
report you to the HOA because your trash can was visible for nine seconds,
glare at you because your wind chimes "offended their energy,"
measure your grass with the intensity of a government contractor,

leave parking notes clearly written after pacing angrily for 45 minutes,
complain about your barking dog while theirs sounds like it's undergoing an exorcism,
call the city because your Christmas lights came down on January 2$^{nd}$.

Petty neighbors wake up every morning ready to ruin someone's day, and they hope it's yours.

These are the final bosses of adulthood.

And they're just getting warmed up.

This is why we can't have nice things.

## Passive-Aggressive Neighbors: Conflict Avoidance with Olympic Precision

Passive-aggressive neighbors don't talk - they communicate through notes.

Notes with perfect handwriting and a tone carefully engineered to raise your blood pressure:
"Just a reminder quiet hours start at 9 p.m."
"Your recycling bin was 2 inches over the line! LOL!"
"Friendly suggestion: your car might be parked a tiny bit crooked :)"
"Hi!! Your dog barked for 14 whole seconds yesterday. Thought you should know!!"

These notes always look cheerful but feel like threats.

Some don't even bother with notes - they slam doors, stomp dramatically, or sigh loud enough to register on the Richter scale.

Nothing makes you contemplate crime quite like hearing your neighbor communicate in passive-aggressive Morse code through the wall.

This is why we can't have nice things.

## The 3 A.M. Mystery Activities

There is something about 3 a.m. that transforms neighbors from ordinary people into cryptids.

At 3 a.m., neighbors suddenly feel compelled to:
vacuum,
rearrange furniture,
drag heavy objects,
start laundry,
blast 2002 club music,
whisper-fight,
loudly "whisper" while drunk,
run on treadmills,
stomp like they're practicing for a medieval battle.

You wake up to BOOM - a sound you cannot identify.

Your brain's theories, in order:
bowling balls,
bodies,
IKEA furniture,
ghosts.
Are you the ghost?

No answers. Just more noises.

This is why we can't have nice things.

# Neighbors Are a High-Stakes Lottery With No Winners

Buying or renting a home is essentially blindfolded roulette. You'll never truly know who lives next to you until it's too late.

Your cast of possible neighbors includes:
The dawn-patrol lawnmower guy.
The late-night "band rehearsal" guy.
The scream-fighting couple who learned nothing from therapy.
The chain-smoking porch philosopher.
The amateur mechanic with six cars and zero mufflers.
The family whose children communicate exclusively through sprinting.
The person who grills constantly and sets off alarms weekly.
The woman who yells at squirrels with unsettling passion.
The shady neighbor who stares through blinds like you're a nature documentary.

Even if you move - new neighbors, new nightmare.
There is always at least one unhinged person within hearing distance, and they always reveal themselves at the worst possible moment.

This is why we can't have nice things.

## Why This Chapter Matters

Neighbors are the daily, close-range version of everything that frustrates you about modern life.

The noise.
The inconsideration.
The emotional chaos.
The unpredictable human nonsense.

It's all right there - six feet from your sanity.

Neighbors take the broad societal dysfunction from Part I and shrink it down until it rattles your walls at 3 a.m. They're the reminder that the problems "out there" don't stay out there. They follow you home. They live next door. They share a wall.
Every slammed door, every midnight thud, every petty note, every yard complaint is a micro-lesson in the emotional climate we all live in:

People are stressed.
People are overwhelmed.
People are weird.
People are loud.
People are barely holding it together.

And when you understand that?

You start to understand why daily life feels like a slow-drip headache with Wi-Fi.

This chapter matters because it shows the transition from *system-level frustration* to *people-level frustration* - the exact bridge that carries you into the rest of Part II.

Neighbors are the first reminder that adulthood is an endurance sport.

This is why we can't have nice things.

# CHAPTER 13 - HOA Rules and Other Forms of Petty Tyranny

There are many forms of organized oppression in this world, but none are as personal, petty, or disproportionately powerful as a homeowners association. HOAs are living proof that you don't need tanks, propaganda, or a throne to rule with absolute authority. You just need a clipboard, a laminated rulebook, and a burning desire to micromanage someone else's landscaping.

People think dictatorships begin with military coups.
No.
They begin with a neighbor in a visor clicking a pen while inspecting your hedges.

This is why we can't have nice things.

## The Cult of Grass-Length Policing

If there is one thing HOAs worship with religious devotion, it's grass length.

They don't just like short grass - they revere it.
They want lawns so uniform they could pass a military inspection. Some dictators in history cared less about conformity than a suburban yard committee.

Rain? Weather? Seasons?
HOAs don't recognize these natural phenomena.

If your grass grows half an inch too long because the Earth did what the Earth does, the HOA treats it like a federal crime. You'll wake up to a notice taped to your door like the FBI is about to raid your begonias:

"Your lawn does not meet the community's aesthetic standards."

Neither does the rest of the neighborhood, Linda, but here we are.

HOAs act like they're guardians of suburban beauty while they:
measure your turf like CSI agents,
fine you because the sun dared to exist,
treat a single dandelion like a sign of moral collapse.

Nuclear facilities have fewer regulations than some HOA lawns.

This is why we can't have nice things.

## Trash Can Curfews: Petty Tyranny at Its Finest

If you want to understand the psychology of an HOA, examine how it treats trash cans.

Trash cans have stricter time windows than parolees:
Not visible before 7 p.m. the night before pickup.
Must be returned by 9 a.m. sharp.
Must face forward, but not too forward.
Must be stored like contraband behind your house, behind a fence, behind a spiritual barrier.

If a windstorm knocks your bin over - an act of God Himself - the HOA will fine you like you personally insulted the community's ancestors.

"Control the weather... or pay $50."

Trash can rules are HOA psychological warfare.

This is why we can't have nice things.

## The HOA President: Suburban Dictator-in-Chief

Every HOA has That Person - the president who rules with the enthusiasm of someone who finally found an arena where their power matters.

This is the person who:
carries a clipboard like a royal scepter,
quotes bylaws like scripture,
uses phrases like "community integrity" unironically,
believes regulating mailbox color prevents societal collapse,
introduces themselves as "The HOA President" - as if anyone asked.

These people couldn't get respect at work or at home, so they harvest it from strangers who just want to mow their yard in peace.

They don't enforce rules - they weaponize them.

This is why we can't have nice things.

## HOA Board Meetings: Community Theater for the Unhinged

Attend one HOA meeting and your faith in humanity will evaporate.

These meetings include:
drama,

yelling,
conspiracy theories,
middle-aged power struggles,
Ron complaining about parking every month,
Doris clutching the bylaws like holy scripture,
financial reports that no one understands,
one guy who clearly came to fight.

HOA meetings are political theater for people who peaked in high school student government.

You'll always find:

**1. The Rule Lover**
Knows every bylaw, comma, and footnote. Speaks in article numbers. Probably sleeps with the handbook under their pillow.

**2. The Angry Old Guy**
Starts every sentence with "Back in MY day…" and ends every sentence with "…that's why we need stricter enforcement."

**3. The New Couple Who Regret Moving Here**
Showed up thinking they'd "get involved."
Now they're pricing cabins in Montana.

**4. The Treasurer Who Loves Numbers Too Much**
Announces financial updates like they're stock market crashes.

**5. The Person Who Has No Idea Why They're There**
Came for snacks. Stayed for chaos. Will never return.

**6. The HOA Karen**
The suburban Voldemort. The nightmare in capri pants. The reason aspirin sales stay high.

And every meeting ends with zero solutions, rising tension, and someone threatening to "take this to the city council," as if the city council gives a single damn about Gary's noncompliant pergola.

This is why we can't have nice things.

## The HOA Karen: The Neighborhood's Self-Appointed Secret Police

If the president is the dictator, the HOA Karen is the enforcement arm.

She possesses:
binoculars,
heightened hearing,
an internal alarm for rule violations,
a strong sense of personal injustice,
a deep love for the phrase "I'm going to report this."

She patrols the neighborhood with a tiny dog and the righteousness of a medieval inquisitor.

She will:
measure your lawn,
glare at your holiday decorations,
file complaints about your curtains,
take photos of your trash can placement,
leave notes that start with "As a member of this community...."

HOA Karens believe they are preserving civilization.
In reality, they are the #1 cause of neighborhood strife.

This is why we can't have nice things.

## Minor Violations Treated Like War Crimes

No one escalates like an HOA.

Harmless things become international incidents:
A birdbath that's 2 inches too tall,
A holiday decoration lingering 12 hours after the holiday,
A gnome facing the wrong direction,
Curtains that aren't "community neutral,"
An RV in the driveway for 24 hours,
A garage door left open too long,
A child's toy visible from the street,
A flag not officially approved by the board.

To the HOA, this isn't a minor oversight - you've endangered the fragile fabric of society.

This is why we can't have nice things.

## The HOA Newsletter: Passive-Aggression in Monthly Form

HOA newsletters always include:
cheerful clip art,
veiled threats,
overly positive messages dripping with judgment,
reminders no one needed,
financial updates no one understands,
"community events" no one attends.

Everything is just a little too cheerful - the suburban equivalent of a customer service rep smiling while hating you deeply.

Examples:

"Let's keep our yards tidy!"
Translation: Someone's yard looks like a feral goat attacked it.

"Please place trash cans out only during approved hours!"
Translation: We know what you did.

"Friendly reminder: decorations must be seasonally appropriate!"
Translation: Your pumpkin in February made Karen cry.

HOA newsletters are propaganda with exclamation points.

This is why we can't have nice things.

## HOA Logic: Wrong, But Extremely Confident

HOAs operate under one consistent principle:

If it inconveniences you, it will be enforced.
If it helps you, it's not in the bylaws.

They preach community but enforce conformity.
They praise individuality but punish uniqueness.
They claim to protect property values but mostly protect feelings.

And none of it needs to make sense.

They don't need to be right.
They just need to be in charge.

This is why we can't have nice things.

# Why This Chapter Matters

HOAs are more than an inconvenience.
They're a miniature model of everything that drives people insane about modern adulthood.

The control.
The surveillance.
The arbitrary rules.
The power trips.
The people who desperately need a meaningful outlet and choose… your lawn.

HOAs take the small stresses of daily life and institutionalize them. They transform normal neighbors into frustrated, defensive, emotionally exhausted versions of themselves - all because someone decided a trash can was visible for six minutes too long.

They turn minor problems into moral failures.
They turn communities into battlegrounds.
They turn "home" - the one place that's supposed to be peaceful - into a place where you're constantly waiting for the next notice, the next complaint, the next ridiculous rule.

And that's why this chapter matters:

HOAs aren't just about grass length or trash cans.
They represent the creeping, everyday bureaucracy that erodes patience, autonomy, and sanity.
They show how quickly power can escalate when the wrong people get a clipboard.
They illustrate how modern life is full of tiny, relentless pressures that chip away at us until we don't even notice we're grinding our teeth.

Living under an HOA forces you to confront a universal truth about adulthood:

You're always one letter, one meeting, or one neighborhood Karen away from losing your mind.

This is why we can't have nice things.

# CHAPTER 14 - Traffic: A Social Experiment Gone Wrong

Traffic is more than cars on roads - it's the greatest psychological experiment ever conducted on the American people without consent. Every day, millions of otherwise decent humans climb into two-ton metal boxes and immediately reveal how terrible we are collectively as a species.

If you want to understand society, politics, culture, or human behavior, you don't need a sociology degree. You just need a 20-minute commute.

Traffic turns calm people into lunatics, reasonable people into screamers, and mild-mannered adults into creatures who mutter "I swear to God..." forty-seven times before they reach the next light.

No matter who you are, where you live, or what you drive… you hate everyone else on the road.

And nowhere is the phrase more accurate than here:

This is why we can't have nice things.

## Nobody in America Knows How to Merge

If aliens landed and watched Americans attempt to merge, they would leave immediately and file a report declaring Earth uninhabitable due to "terminal stupidity."

Merging is extremely simple. It is literally:

"You go, then I go."

But in America, merging is a blood sport. A gladiator arena. Darwinism with turn signals.

You've got:
The Speed-Up-At-All-Costs Psycho.
The On-Ramp Sloth.
The Absolutely-Not-Letting-You-In Warrior.
The Lane-Ends-Now Daredevil.
The Full Stop On-Ramp Menace.

Two cars. One lane.
Limitless stupidity.

Merging exposes the darkest depths of the human soul.

This is why we can't have nice things.

---

# Left-Lane Campers: America's Most Hated Subspecies

Left-lane campers are the final boss of American driving.

The left lane is for passing - not reflection, sightseeing, or emotional healing.

But these people cruise along at the exact speed limit as if they're guiding a mindfulness seminar.

They know what they're doing.
They simply do not care.

Their excuses:

"I'm going fast enough."
"They can go around."
"I have the right to be here."

Yes. You technically do.
And I technically have the right to scream into my steering wheel like a Shakespearean widow.

Left-lane campers ruin lives.

This is why we can't have nice things.

## The Psychology of Road Rage

Road rage isn't a flaw.
It's the body's natural response to driving in America.

Driving requires:
trusting strangers who barely passed physics,
believing other people's brakes work,
and having faith in humanity - which is misplaced.

Because you're trapped in a metal box with no escape, the smallest offense feels like a personal attack:
late blinker,
slow left turn,
sudden brake tap,
rolling stop,
someone drifting into your lane "just to check."

Your body treats these like mortal threats because on some level...
they are.

This is why we can't have nice things.

# City Drivers vs. Rural Drivers

America has two distinct driving cultures:
those forged in chaos, and those raised in cornfields.

## City Drivers

Aggressive. Scarred. Running on caffeine and rage.

They:
honk before the light turns green,
change lanes like they're teleporting,
treat speed limits like optional décor.

## Rural Drivers

Calm. Friendly. Unpredictable in ways that defy physics.

They:
wave at literally everyone,
brake for butterflies,
turn without signaling because "everybody knows where I'm goin'."

When these two species meet?
Civilization collapses.

This is why we can't have nice things.

# Driver Types You Meet (A Field Guide to American Road Lunacy)

Spend one hour on American roads and you'll encounter at least a dozen of these creatures:

**The Turn-Signal Denier** - believes indicators are a government conspiracy.
If their blinker ever turns on, it's by accident and they panic.

**The Braker-for-Nothing** - stops for ghosts.
Invisible hazards only they can see.

**The Lane Drifter** - spiritually adrift, physically adrift.
Their car moves like their soul: without purpose.

**The Blinker-Left-On Traveler** - signaling since the Obama administration.
Will die before turning it off.

**The Thursday Sunday Driver** - moves like it's a peaceful weekend no matter what day it is.
Chaos behind them. Serenity in their heart.

**The Absolutely-Not-Letting-You-In Warrior** - merge? over their dead body.
They treat lane transitions like contested land.

**The Last-Second Lane Changer** - suicidal confidence.
They believe luck IS a driving strategy.

**The "I'll Merge When I'm Damn Ready" Rebel** - timing is a social construct.
Merge signs are merely suggestions.

**The Tailgater** - wants to ride in your backseat.
If they get any closer, they'll owe you child support.

**The High-Beam Hero** - blinds you into a religious experience.
Sees darkness as a personal insult.

**The Rolling Subwoofer** - shares their playlist with the entire zip code.
If your rearview mirror isn't vibrating, they're not happy.

**The Multi-Tasker** - eating, texting, steering with a knee.
A Cirque du Soleil act on wheels.

**The Overly Cautious Grandma** - braking for the *idea* of braking.
A leaf blows across the road and she repents her sins.

**The Speed-Up-At-All-Costs Psycho** - sees your turn signal and floors it.
They'd rather die than let you merge.

**The On-Ramp Sloth** - enters the freeway at 22 mph.
Believes acceleration is a form of arrogance.

**The Overcompensating Truck Guy** - louder than his self-esteem.
His exhaust system cost more than his emotional development.

**The Minivan Missile** - late for soccer. Prepared for war.
A deceptively wholesome vehicle piloted by pure rage.

**The Diagonal Parker** - takes two spots like it's a hobby.
Every parking lot is their personal art gallery.

**The Rules-Don't-Apply-To-Me Lunatic** - parks on medians, sidewalks, and probably feelings.
A sovereign citizen of chaos.

**The Underpowered Car** - accelerates like a depression-era toaster.
Their top speed is "eventually."

**The Rage Screamer** - full therapy session behind the wheel.
You don't hear words. You hear trauma.

**The Spiritually Guided Parker** - parks wherever the universe leads them.
Lines are optional. Geometry? A suggestion.

**The Brake-Check Prophet** - taps their brakes to "teach lessons" no one asked for.
Creating chaos one ego trip at a time.

**The Backup-Camera Denier** - owns one; refuses to use it.
Prefers the raw human experience of guessing.

**The Throttle Philosopher** - coasts through life and intersections.
Deep thoughts. Zero urgency.

**The Normal Driver** - fictional. Possibly extinct.
Scientists believe they once existed during the early 1990s.

This is why we can't have nice things.

## Roundabouts: America's Kryptonite

If you want to watch Americans short-circuit in real time, introduce a roundabout.

Roundabouts are simple.
But in America, they function as chaos circles.

Disasters include:
The Accelerator of Doom - enters at full speed without looking.
The Roundabout Statue - refuses to enter the circle under any circumstances.
The Opposite-Direction Adventurer - spiritually and physically lost.

Communities debate roundabouts like they're debating constitutional amendments:

"Are they safe?"
"Are they socialist?"
"Do they reduce freedom?"

Americans fear roundabouts the way cats fear cucumbers.

This is why we can't have nice things.

## People Who Can't Park: A National Emergency

If you want proof civilization is collapsing, go to any grocery store parking lot.

Parking is a basic task.
Most people fail miserably.

The Offenders:
The Diagonal Disaster - takes up two spaces flawlessly.
The Close Enough Artist - crooked, halfway in, halfway out.
The Compact Car Performance Artist - needs 14 attempts.
The Massive Truck Guy - three spaces, still crooked.
The Crooked Quitter - saw it was bad and just left.
The Shopping Cart Anarchist - leaves carts roaming like feral animals.
The Spiritually Guided Parker - picks any surface that feels right.
The Backer-Inner - takes forever, proud of themselves.
The Parallel Panic Attack - attempts once, drives away defeated.

Parking lots are society's report card.
We're failing.

This is why we can't have nice things.

# Traffic Isn't Just a Mess - It's a Mirror

Driving exposes the truth about Americans:
we lack patience,
we lack communication,
we lack self-awareness,
and we absolutely believe everyone else is the problem.

Traffic is the world's largest personality test - and America consistently scores "needs improvement."

# Why This Chapter Matters

Traffic is the daily reminder that society is held together with duct tape, wishful thinking, and whatever shred of patience people have left before 8 a.m.

It exposes everything we pretend isn't true about humanity:
that we're impatient,
that we're selfish,
that we're terrible at sharing anything,
and that the idea of "common sense" was clearly a myth we made up to feel better.

On the road, the mask comes off.
There's no polite smile,
no forced small talk,
no pretending we're reasonable adults.

It's just you,
your blood pressure,
and a parade of complete strangers making decisions that should be and probably are, illegal.

Merging becomes a moral crisis.

Parking becomes performance art.
Roundabouts become trauma.
A left-lane camper becomes a personal betrayal.

Traffic doesn't just frustrate us -
it reveals us.

It magnifies all the little flaws people keep hidden in everyday life:
the entitlement,
the obliviousness,
the refusal to think two seconds ahead,
the absolute certainty that everyone else is the problem.

This chapter matters because driving forces you to confront the truth:
if we can't cooperate for five consecutive seconds on a public road,
how the hell are we supposed to function anywhere else?

Every commute is a social experiment.
Every mile is a psychological test.
Every idiot who forgets their blinker is a message from the universe.

And every single time someone parks diagonally, merges like a daredevil, or comes to a complete stop on an on-ramp, you're reminded of the only conclusion that makes sense:

This is why we can't have nice things.

# CHAPTER 15 - Airports and Airlines: The Ninth Circle of Hell

Air travel used to be glamorous. People dressed nicely. Seats reclined more than an inch. You could eat without wondering whether the food violated the Geneva Conventions.

Now? Flying is an endurance test designed by bureaucratic sadists. Airports and airlines aren't just inconvenient - they are the closest modern equivalent to Dante's ninth circle of hell, complete with suffering, confusion, endless lines, and people who immediately lose 40 IQ points upon entering a terminal.

The moment you walk through the sliding doors, the air feels stale, the lighting is somehow both dim and blinding, and the entire building smells like a mix of Cinnabon, jet fuel, and carpet fibers that last saw a vacuum during the Bush administration.

You haven't even checked a bag yet, and you're already thinking:

This is why we can't have nice things.

## TSA: Theater of Suffering and Futility

TSA is the government's most elaborate performance-art installation: "What If Security... But Pointless?"

No one is good at TSA.
No one is prepared.

No one reads the signs posted every five feet.

People still argue about:
shoes,
laptops,
pockets,
water bottles,
and the 3.4-ounce liquid rule that has existed since the dawn of recorded time.

There's always someone who tries to sneak through a Costco-sized shampoo bottle, then gasps like an innocent martyr when stopped.

TSA agents, meanwhile, fall into two categories:
The Aggressive Yeller - shouting contradictory instructions,
The Silent Watcher - observing you like you're smuggling nuclear secrets in your granola bar.

TSA isn't security.
TSA is a public stress simulator with uniforms.

This is why we can't have nice things.

## People Who Forget How Lines Work

Airports turn normal people into confused cattle.

You'll see:
The 12-Foot Gapper,
The Personal-Space Assassin,
The Wanderer Asking "Is This the Line?,"
The Sociopath Who Thinks "I'm in a Hurry" Overrides Society.

Boarding areas are even worse. Airlines create 47 different boarding groups that mean absolutely nothing because the moment a gate agent says any word starting with "B" - boarding, beginning, biscotti - half the waiting area springs to life like they've been summoned by a game show host.

## Boarding Groups - The Illusion of Order

Airlines pretend they have systems.
They do not.

They call:
Priority,
Preferred,
Premium,
Platinum,
Ultra Platinum,
Diamond Elite,
Sapphire,
Group 1,
Group A,
Group A-1,
Families,
Military,
"Anyone breathing."

EVERYONE stands.

Boarding groups aren't order.

They're psychological experiments measuring how quickly human beings will ignore instructions. The answer: nine seconds.

Any time a gate agent says "Please wait until your group is called" and the crowd surges forward anyway?

You know exactly where you are...

This is why we can't have nice things.

## Carry-On Wars: A Battle of Wits (Nobody Wins)

Once on the jet bridge, the real war begins: the fight for overhead bin space.

People bring "carry-ons" roughly the size of refrigerators, then attempt to cram them overhead using the force of a hydraulic press.

You meet:
The Overhead Hog,
The Stuffer,
The Gate-Check Martyr,
The Personal-Item Hoarder (with four personal items).

The flight attendant says,
"Smaller bags under the seat, please."
No one listens.
It's the Hunger Games with luggage.

## The Time I Almost Committed Airborne Homicide

On a flight to Denver, I watched a man halt the entire boarding process because he REFUSED to gate-check his grotesquely oversized carry-on - a suitcase the size of a 1990s desktop computer tower with wheels large enough for agricultural use.

The attendant gently said,

"Sir, it won't fit."
He confidently replied,
"Oh, it'll fit."

Then he began a five-minute interpretive dance:
lifting,
ramming,
twisting,
stuffing,
praying,
pushing,
shoving.

It. Did. Not. Fit.

When it finally became undeniable, he turned around and glared at the rest of us like we were the reason physics betrayed him.

This man helped me understand how people end up on no-fly lists.

This is why we can't have nice things.

## Airline Seats: Torture Devices With Seatbelts

Modern airline seats are engineered by people who have never met a human spine.

Your options include:
2 inches of foam,
0.7 inches of recline,
legroom measured in units smaller than millimeters.

Middle seats?
Cruel and unusual punishment.

Anyone who willingly takes the middle seat deserves sainthood and monetary compensation.

Airlines advertise "extra legroom" like it's a luxury - not a basic requirement for circulation.

This is why we can't have nice things.

# Delays That Materialize Out of Thin Air

The greatest mystery in modern aviation is how a flight listed as "On Time" can instantly transform into a six-hour delay.

Reasons include:
"Mechanical issues,"
"Weather" (in a state you're not traveling to),
"Crew timing,"
"Paperwork,"
"Operational circumstances" (vague enough to be anything from a missing bolt to divine intervention).

Delay times shift like lottery numbers:

On time → 20 min → 2 hours → 40 min → 3 hours → "awaiting update" → "we don't know where the plane is."

How do you misplace a plane?

Passengers don't get angry after a while - they simply deflate.
Everyone adopts the same expression:
The hollow, resigned stare of people who've accepted their fate.

This is why we can't have nice things.

# Why This Chapter Matters

Airports and airlines aren't just inconvenient - they are a concentrated microcosm of everything broken in modern life.

Nowhere else do you see humanity collapse so quickly or so consistently.
People forget how lines work.
Rules dissolve.
Logic evaporates.
Adults become confused toddlers with rolling suitcases.

Flying exposes the truth we avoid in daily life:
we are overwhelmed, impatient, disorganized, easily agitated, and absolutely convinced we're the only ones doing things correctly.

Every TSA shuffle, every boarding-group riot, every overhead-bin battle, every sudden six-hour delay shows how thin our patience is… and how quickly it snaps.

Airports reveal how fragile the idea of "order" really is.
One announcement, one rule, one inconvenience - and the entire terminal melts into chaos.

This chapter matters because air travel magnifies the flaws we pretend aren't there:
the selfishness,
the confusion,
the entitlement,
the performative outrage,
the total lack of self-awareness.

It's the ultimate test of human cooperation -
and we fail spectacularly.

And every time someone holds up the security line, argues about boarding zones, tries to cram a refrigerator-sized carry-on overhead, or sighs loudly at the departure board like it personally betrayed them...

You can't help but remember:

This is why we can't have nice things.

# CHAPTER 16 - Workplace Nonsense and Other Corporate Fairy Tales

There is a universal truth in America:
Workplaces would run better if fewer people actually tried to run them.

Corporate life is a bizarre social ecosystem filled with contradictions, pointless rituals, and people who use phrases like "circle back" with a straight face. It's a world where grown adults spend their days pretending to be busy, pretending to care, and pretending the company mission statement matters more than their desire to go home.

Every workplace - big or small, corporate or nonprofit, office or remote - follows the same pattern: endless meetings, fake positivity, HR overreach, buzzwords nobody understands, software that actively sabotages you, and a complete disregard for anything resembling real productivity.

Walking into your job some days feels like stepping into a live-action parody of adulthood, and every hour that passes reminds you:

This is why we can't have nice things.

## Meetings: The Black Hole of Productivity

There is nothing more destructive to human progress than a meeting.

Meetings are where ideas go to die.

Meetings exist for one reason: because someone in management doesn't trust employees to work unless they're being watched on video chat.

Most meetings fall into at least one of these categories:

**The Meeting That Could Have Been an Email**
Ninety percent of meetings live here.
People gather, talk in circles, nod a lot, and leave with no plan, no decisions, and no will to keep living.

**The Update Meeting With No Updates**
Everyone takes turns saying some variation of:
"Nothing new on my end."
So why are we here?

**The Meeting Before the Meeting**
A warm-up session for the "real" meeting, which will also achieve nothing.

**The "Quick 15-Minute" Meeting That Steals an Hour of Your Life**
A crime, honestly.

**The Manager Who Shares Their Screen and Clicks Slowly**
Every click feels like a new chapter of your life passing by.

**The Brainstorm Run by the Most Annoying Person Alive**
"Ideation sessions" led by people who have never had an idea worth writing down.

Meanwhile, actual work sits unattended like a sad plant in the corner.

Meetings aren't for productivity - they're for management cosplay.

And every time a new calendar invite appears, you already know:

This is why we can't have nice things.

## Corporate Buzzwords: The Language of the Delusional

Corporate America has invented an entire dialect of nonsense - a language so vague and inflated that no one outside a boardroom would ever speak it voluntarily.

Buzzwords exist to disguise the fact that nothing meaningful is happening.

Some of the worst offenders:
"Circle back" - I'll ignore you until you remind me.
"Leverage synergies" - Two words that mean nothing together.
"Bandwidth" - You're a human, not a router.
"Thought leadership" - Posting on LinkedIn.
"Low-hanging fruit" - Stop talking about fruit.
"Going forward" - As opposed to… going backward?
"Pivot" - Panic, but with optimism.
"Client-centric outcomes" - We have no idea what we're doing.


Imagine ordering lunch in corporate jargon:

"Let's leverage our hunger bandwidth and align on a sandwich-centric solution."

You'd be removed from the premises.

Corporate jargon is the duct tape holding together the illusion that anyone knows what's going on.

This is why we can't have nice things.

## Fake Positivity Culture: Please Smile While Everything Burns

Modern workplaces love "positivity."

Not real positivity - the forced, manic kind where management demands enthusiasm while giving employees absolutely nothing to be enthusiastic about.

This is the era of:
motivational posters,
"fun" team-building exercises,
corporate wellness initiatives,
forced bonding activities,
and appreciation emails that end with "Thank you for all you do!" but never with a raise.

Companies love saying:

"We're a family!"

No. We're not.
Families help each other.
Companies give you lukewarm Costco pizza instead of benefits.

Or:

"Your mental health matters!"

Right before dropping 47 tasks on you with a 3 p.m. deadline.

The classic:

"Let's make this our best quarter ever!"

Buddy, I barely survived last quarter. Please relax.

Fake positivity is just corporate gaslighting with balloons.

This is why we can't have nice things.

## HR: The Department of No

Human Resources should, in theory, help humans.

Instead, HR is the Department of No - a bureaucracy designed to protect the company, delay solutions, and avoid lawsuits while providing zero emotional support.

Want a raise? No.
Better equipment? No.
Clearer policies? No.
Want the toxic coworker fired? Absolutely not - they've been here too long.

HR speaks in carefully rehearsed phrases like:
"We take this very seriously."
"We'll investigate."
"Thank you for bringing this to our attention."
"Per policy…"

Then nothing happens.

HR is the HOA of the workplace: obsessed with rules, allergic to common sense, and determined to ruin the simplest requests.

This is why we can't have nice things.

## Virtual Meeting Software - The Digital Hellscape We Pretend Is Useful

If Dante were alive today, he'd rewrite hell into a single circle called virtual meetings.

Virtual Meeting Software:
freezes for no reason,
delivers messages out of order,
sends notifications three days late,
and acts like it has never seen the conversation you're literally looking at.

Every virtual meeting begins with the same ritual:

"Can you hear me?"
"You're muted."
"Now we can't hear you."
"You sound like a robot."
"Why am I echoing?"
"Who has an echo?"

Then someone shares their screen and their computer instantly boots into Windows 95 mode.

Virtual meeting software isn't collaboration.
Virtual meetings programs are a digital cry for help disguised as software.

This is why we can't have nice things.

# Email - The Eternal Curse of Modern Work

Email is where productivity goes to die.

Your inbox is a graveyard of:
passive-aggressive "per my last email" attacks,
walls of text written like legal filings,
reply-all criminals,
midnight senders who hate boundaries,
and threads that turn into 57-message sagas with no resolution.

Email isn't communication.

Email is a chore.

Nothing good ever arrives by email.

If something good DID arrive by email, you'd assume it was a phishing scam.

There should be a law that you're allowed to lightly slap anyone who sends a "Just circling back!" follow-up less than 24 hours after the first message.

And every time your unread count jumps from 5 to 83 in under five minutes, you know:

This is why we can't have nice things.

# Performance Reviews - The Corporate Horoscope

Performance reviews are the most pointless ritual in corporate life - a yearly ceremony where your manager writes a fictional short story about who they think you are, and you pretend it's accurate so you don't get fired.

Performance reviews are corporate horoscopes:
vaguely flattering,
deeply unhelpful,
and completely disconnected from reality.

You'll read lines like:

"You're doing great, but there's always room to grow."

Translation:
We will not be giving you a raise.

Or:

"You exceeded expectations in several key areas."

Translation:
We needed to fill space.

Or the classic:

"We encourage you to take more initiative!"

Translation:
Please do more work for the same pay.

Performance reviews rate you on:

"team spirit,"
"engagement,"
"alignment with values,"
"strategic thinking,"
and "professional enthusiasm,"

- none of which are in your job description.

And then, after 700 words of vague nonsense, your manager clicks the same box every year:

"Meets Expectations."

Performance reviews aren't assessments.
They're paperwork so management can claim they "developed their people."

This is why we can't have nice things.

## Corporate Fairy Tales: The Lies We All Pretend to Believe

Every job has its sacred myths - the bedtime stories we all collectively pretend to believe:
promotions are earned,
leadership values feedback,
work-life balance exists,
the company cares,
raises are coming "next quarter,"
and open-door policies mean anything.

Corporate fairy tales are the emotional bubble wrap keeping the whole system from collapsing.
We smile.
We nod.

We pretend.

Because the alternative is chaos.

And every time a manager says, "We're a family," while quietly planning layoffs, you realize again:

This is why we can't have nice things.

## Why This Chapter Matters

Work shouldn't be this hard.
Not the tasks - the nonsense surrounding the tasks.

Corporate life reveals the absurdity baked into modern adulthood:
endless meetings,
fake positivity,
pointless jargon,
HR theatrics,
broken software,
and the constant pressure to look busy while accomplishing absolutely nothing.

Workplaces don't fall apart because of the work.
They fall apart because of the systems built around the work -
the rituals, the politics, the circling back, the aligning, the pivoting, the bandwidth-checking, the calendar invites that multiply like bacteria.

Every job becomes a psychological obstacle course where people are expected to smile, collaborate, innovate, engage, synergize, and "lean in" while drowning in inefficiency.

This chapter matters because the workplace is where most adults spend the majority of their waking lives -

and instead of being functional, it's an elaborate performance held together with buzzwords, outdated software, and collective delusion.

It shows how easily structure becomes chaos.
How quickly professionalism becomes parody.
How workplaces pretend to value humans while systematically exhausting them.

Corporate life is the ultimate reminder that adulthood is not logical - it's theatrical.

And every meeting that should've been an email,
every HR script delivered with dead-eyed enthusiasm,
every performance review full of fictional compliments,
every software crash,
every forced "team-building" event,
every jargon-laden memo,
and every pointless process reinforces the same truth:

This is why we can't have nice things.

# CHAPTER 17 - Five-Minute Tasks That Somehow Take Two Hours

There are certain tasks in life that should take five minutes.

Should.

But we live in America, where nothing is simple, nothing is efficient, and every small chore somehow turns into a bureaucratic obstacle course designed by a bored demon with a clipboard.

We've all had those innocent, hopeful moments where you think:

"I'll just get this done real quick,"

…and suddenly it's dark outside, you've aged emotionally, you're sweating for reasons you can't identify, and you've been transferred to your sixth customer service representative, all of whom are "just trying their best."

This chapter is dedicated to those deceptively small tasks that morph into multi-hour odysseys - the ones that make you question society, technology, your own sanity, and the structural integrity of whatever object is currently betraying you.

Every single one ends the same way:

This is why we can't have nice things.

# Calling Customer Service: A Journey Into Madness

Calling customer service is modern psychological warfare.

You don't just call a number - you willingly step into an emotional escape room with no clues, no exits, and no survivors.

It starts with the phone tree.

A robotic voice greets you with the same lie you've heard your whole life:

"Please listen carefully, as our menu options have changed."

No they haven't.
They never have.
This message is corporate folklore.

Then the options:
"Press 1 for billing."
"Press 2 for technical support."
"Press 3 for all other inquiries."
"Press 4 to hear these options again because you blacked out in frustration."

You press 2.
The robot cheerfully replies:

"Okay! Connecting you to billing."

Then comes the scream into the void:

"REPRESENTATIVE! HUMAN! AGENT!"

The robot answers:

"I think you said you'd like to hear about our new promotions."

By the time you reach an actual person - someone named Kyle, in a call center that sounds like a hurricane full of printers and coughing - you've lost the will to live.

Kyle asks for your name, birthdate, address, last four digits of your soul, and the color of the shirt you wore in high school graduation photos. Then he puts you on hold "just for a moment."

You wait long enough to re-evaluate your entire life.
He returns only to say:

"Let me transfer you."

Kyle, you traitor.

The department he transfers you to?
Closed 45 minutes ago.

You hang up, defeated, whispering to no one:

This is why we can't have nice things.

## "Quick Errands": The Ultimate Lie

"I'll just run a quick errand," you say.

Famous last words.

A "quick errand" is a fantasy. A delusion. A lie we tell ourselves to get out the door.

You walk into the store and immediately regret your choices. People are moving at three miles per century. Someone is on FaceTime loudly discussing their gallbladder. A toddler isn't crying - they're screaming like a tiny demon doing vocal warmups.

You just want ONE thing.

Milk? It's in the back, past the construction zone, behind a pallet of mystery product.

Need a specific tool at the hardware store? They moved it. Nobody knows where. The guy in the apron says, "We don't carry that," while standing directly in front of a giant display labeled exactly what you asked for.

Need stamps at the post office? Hope you packed rations. The line is long enough to induce an existential crisis.

Then checkout begins:
Self-checkout freezes like it saw a ghost.
Someone is arguing over expired coupons from 2014.
An elderly man is paying in pennies earned during the Reagan administration.
The card reader decides YOUR card is suddenly a security threat.

Your "quick errand" has now qualified as a saga.

This is why we can't have nice things.

## Phone Trees From Hell: Design Flaw or Conspiracy?

Phone trees are not customer service tools - they're psychological experiments to see how long it takes before an adult screams into a phone.

Check the call log after one of these nightmares:
Call time: 1 hour 48 minutes,
Actual human interaction: 6 minutes.

The rest is:
"Please hold."
"Your call is important to us." (It's not.)
"Estimated wait time is… 52 minutes."
"We are experiencing unusually high call volume." (They always are.)

You say clearly:
"Billing."
Robot:
"I heard 'technical support.' Connecting you now."

No you didn't.
You heard nothing. You're not even alive.

Eventually you reach a human who politely informs you they cannot solve your issue and you must go - full circle - right back to the automated system that sent you here.

In that moment, you understand ancient rage on a cellular level.

This is why we can't have nice things.

## Anything Involving a Printer: A Technological Curse

Printers are cursed objects. There is no other explanation.

Everything else in technology has evolved: phones, computers, cars, appliances. Hell, even toothbrushes got smart.

Printers, though?

Printers are still possessed by the same demon from 1998.

You need to print ONE PAGE.

The printer responds by:
jamming,
running out of ink,
announcing "Error code 409,"
claiming it's offline,
demanding cyan ink even though you're printing black and white,
and insisting on a driver update last installed by Vikings.

Then - randomly, hours later - it prints 14 copies of whatever you tried to print earlier, just to assert dominance.

Printers are proof humanity was never meant to flourish.

This is why we can't have nice things.

## Tasks That Should Be Simple... But Absolutely Aren't

Some tasks seem straightforward.

They SHOULD be.

But America refuses to let anything be easy.

**The DMV**
The DMV exists in a separate dimension where time does not behave normally.
They always need a form you've never heard of.
You always wait an eternity.

You always leave defeated.

**Canceling a Subscription**
Signing up takes 3 seconds.
Canceling requires:
a login,
a password reset,
a hidden menu,
five confirmation screens,
and a guilt trip from "Retention Specialist Kevin."

**Returning Anything**
The return counter is where hope goes to die.
Someone is returning an item purchased during the Clinton era.
The employee types like they're diffusing a bomb.
A manager is summoned by ancient ritual.

**Moving Money Between Your Own Accounts**
It's your money - but banks need 3 - 5 business days to "process" it, like it's aging in a barrel.

**Setting Up a Router**
Plug it in. It fails.
Reset it with a paperclip. It fails.
Call support.
They say, "Try unplugging it again."

Still fails.

This is why we can't have nice things.

# "Five-Minute" Tasks at Work (That Steal Half the Day)

Workplaces specialize in turning tiny tasks into multi-hour catastrophes.

**Logging Into Anything**
Wrong password.
Wrong username.
Two-factor prompts.
Expired codes.
CAPTCHAs with 19 blurry traffic lights.

**Updating One Document**
The file is "locked by another user."
You don't have permission.
Duplicates it for no reason.
The only version you can open is from 2019.

**Sending One Quick Email**
You need an attachment. It's missing.
The server freezes.
I.T. says, "Reboot."
Rebooting closes everything, including the perfect email you just drafted.

**Asking a Quick Question**
You send a chat.
They respond: "Let's hop on a call."
Suddenly you're in a 25-minute meeting about things you never asked.

**Printing at Work**
One printer is jammed.
One is out of toner.
One is "for managers only."

The fourth only prints on alternate Thursdays.

**Restarting Your Computer**
It installs 57 updates, reboots 4 times, and sits on "Just a moment…" for 18 minutes.

**Checking One Thing in a System**
You click. It freezes.
You get kicked out.
I.T. resets your password.
The verification email expires while you're opening it.

**I.T.'s "Quick Fix"**
I.T.: "This'll take five minutes."
Reality: An hour of black screens, confused sighs, and the phrase "Huh. That's weird."

This is why we can't have nice things.

## Why This Chapter Matters

Five-minute tasks aren't just annoying -
they're proof that modern life is held together with zip ties, broken software, and the collective delusion that anything should be simple.

These tiny chores reveal how fragile the entire system is.
Nothing works the way it's supposed to.
Nothing takes the time it should.
And nothing - absolutely nothing - is as straightforward as advertised.

Every call to customer service,
every "quick errand,"
every phone tree detour,
every cursed encounter with a printer,

reminds you that our daily lives depend on processes nobody tested, systems nobody maintains, and rules nobody understands.

This chapter matters because it exposes the truth:
the real exhaustion of adulthood doesn't come from big responsibilities -
it comes from the endless stream of small tasks that steal your time, your patience, and occasionally your will to live.

These aren't just inconveniences.
They are constant, grinding reminders that efficiency is a myth, simplicity is a fairy tale, and the modern world is one minor error code away from total collapse.

Five-minute tasks become two-hour ordeals because the infrastructure of daily life is cracked, chaotic, and designed by people who have never attempted to use it.

And every time a phone tree traps you in a loop,
every time a printer demands cyan ink for a black-and-white page,
every time a "quick" errand turns into a side quest from hell,
you understand - fully, deeply, spiritually - the universal frustration in your bones:

This is why we can't have nice things.

# CHAPTER 18 - The DMV: Bureaucratic Torture With Fluorescent Lighting

There are places on earth that drain your soul: dentist waiting rooms, airport security lines, and certain Walmart's after 10 p.m.
But none compare - NONE - to the DMV.

The DMV isn't a government office.

It's a portal.

A dimension.

A vortex of hopelessness wrapped in flickering fluorescent lighting and the faint smell of expired paperwork.

You step inside and the air changes - heavy, stale, humid with human despair.

Time slows.
Your optimism dies.
Your posture collapses.
You age five years on contact.

And right away, you remember:

This is why we can't have nice things.

# Where Hope Goes to File for an Extension

The DMV is the only place in America where everyone looks like they're attending their own funeral.
People slump in plastic chairs arranged with all the warmth of a hostage negotiation.
Nobody smiles.
Nobody talks.
Nobody looks alive.

Everyone holds some combination of:
paperwork they don't understand,
a number printed on a paper thinner than hospital tissue,
and the unmistakable expression of someone reconsidering their entire life.

A woman clutches a folder thicker than a college textbook.
A man stares into the distance like he's reliving every bad decision he's ever made.
A teenager sits motionless, having already given up on the concept of joy.

If humanity's suffering ever needs to be studied under controlled conditions, researchers shouldn't build a lab - they should rent out a DMV lobby.

# The Ticket System: Designed by Sadists, Powered by Chaos

The number system is not there to help you.
It's there to break you psychologically.

You walk in and pull a number:
A-573.

You look up at the screen:
Now serving A-12.

A. Twelve.

You are going to die here.

The numbers follow no pattern.
The letters follow no rules.
The order obeys only the whims of a malicious universe.

"Now serving B-49."
"Now serving A-13."
"Now serving G-112."

G?
What is G??
Why is 49 before 13?
Why is counter 4 always abandoned like a cursed artifact?

You start decoding the system like it's a CIA cipher.
Civilizations rise and fall before your number moves.

Your coffee gets cold.
Your soul evaporates.

## The Employees: Veterans of a War Against Joy

DMV employees look like they clocked in sometime around the Nixon administration and simply never left.
Not all of them - but enough that the vibe is unmistakable.

You approach the counter.

The clerk greets you with the emotional range of a damp washcloth.

You hand over your documents.
They glance for 0.8 seconds and say:

"This is the wrong form."

Of course it is.
DMV forms are mythical creatures that evolve every 11 minutes.

## The Form That Didn't Exist

I once went in to renew my license - a task that should've taken five minutes.

Should've.

I waited an eternity. Babies cried. Adults cried. A woman whispered to ghosts.

Finally, my number was called.

I proudly handed over my perfectly organized documents. The clerk skimmed them with the enthusiasm of someone reviewing spam.

Then she said the words that haunt me to this day:

"This is outdated. You need the new Form DL-44B."

New?
Since when?
Where?

She pointed to a pamphlet rack containing nothing but dust and sadness.

Another employee shrugged and said, "Try the kiosk."
The kiosk said, OUT OF ORDER, like it had been since 2003.

Back to the front desk.
"Take another number," they said.

Another number.
Another hour.

When I finally reached a different clerk and explained the situation, she blinked twice and said:

"There is no Form DL-44B."

I nearly astral-projected from rage.

After a few keyboard taps she added:

"You didn't need any additional forms. Step to camera 3."

And there I stood, trying to smile for a license photo while spiritually decomposing.

This - THIS - is why people snap.

This is why we can't have nice things.

# Fluorescent Lights: The Slow Drip of Psychological Damage

The lighting in every DMV is the same: buzzing, flickering, institutional, and spiritually abusive.
It drains warmth from your skin and hope from your heart.

This is not illumination.
This is punishment.

## The Forms: A Paperwork Obstacle Course

Nothing at the DMV is simple.
To update your address, you'll need:
three forms,
two proofs of residency,
mail you threw out last week,
and possibly a blood sacrifice.

Half the forms contradict each other.
One still asks for your fax number like it's 1995.
You fill everything out perfectly… only to be told:

"We prefer black ink."

## The Wasted Day Ritual

Nobody "stops by" the DMV.
You prepare for it.

You pack:
snacks,
water,
a phone charger,
emotional fortitude,
maybe a priest.

Still not enough.

A DMV visit always costs the entire day - and a piece of your soul.

## The Exit: Rebirth Through Suffering

Walking out of the DMV feels like escaping from underground captivity.

Sunlight hits your face.
Birds chirp.
Colors exist again.

But deep inside, you know the truth:

You will return someday.
And when you do, your number will again be A-13 while the screen calls G-112.

Because if any place in America proves the central thesis of this entire book, it's this:

This is why we can't have nice things.

## Why This Chapter Matters

The DMV isn't just annoying.
It's a magnifying glass over everything broken, bloated, and backward in modern life.

It's the one place where all the flaws we pretend don't exist - inefficiency, confusion, outdated systems, bad design, pointless bureaucracy, emotional exhaustion - all show up in the same room at the same time.

A DMV visit reveals how fragile the social contract really is.
Lines make no sense.
Forms contradict each other.
Screens blink random letters.

Nobody knows what's happening.
Nobody communicates clearly.
Nobody is happy to be there - not even the employees.

This chapter matters because the DMV is the purest example of what happens when systems outlive logic.
It's a monument to inefficiency.
A shrine to wasted time.
A living museum dedicated to paperwork, confusion, and despair.

Everything that should take five minutes becomes a test of endurance.
Everything simple becomes complicated.
Everything straightforward becomes a scavenger hunt for documents that may not even exist.

The DMV shows us what happens when processes replace people, when rules replace common sense, and when nobody has updated anything since the Carter administration.

It's the ultimate reminder that modern life isn't failing because people are stupid -
it's failing because the systems we rely on are held together with tape, flickering lights, and ancient printers that scream in binary.

And every form mismatch, every number called out of order, every flicker of fluorescent lighting, every kiosk that's "temporarily out of service," and every soul-crushing visit that steals your entire day reinforces the truth:

This is why we can't have nice things.

# CHAPTER 19 - Part-Time Dads and the Parenthood Participation Trophy

There's a special category of men in America:
The ones who treat fatherhood like an optional hobby.

They show up twice a month, post a filtered photo, pay child support *once*, and suddenly believe they've unlocked Father of the Year like it's an Xbox achievement.

These are the Part-Time Dads.
The Weekend Warriors.
The Holiday Heroes.
The Hashtag Fathers.

They want maximum praise for minimum effort, because in their minds parenting works like a loyalty program:

Materialize like a part-time ghost dad enough times and eventually you unlock a free kid.

Meanwhile, the full-time parent - usually the mother - is doing everything:
lunches,
schedules,
homework,
doctor visits,
meltdowns,
activities,
emotional management,

actual parenting,
the whole damn job.

But somehow he's the one applauded for "trying."
This right here?

This is why we can't have nice things.

## The Weekend Warrior Dad

These dads appear exclusively on weekends - and even that's tentative.

On weekends they transform into Fun Dad:
junk food,
zero rules,
pure sugar-fueled chaos.

The kids stay up until midnight.
Breakfast is soda.
Lunch is something microwaved in its original packaging.
Bedtime?
Not his jurisdiction.

But ask him to handle a Tuesday morning drop-off?

"Oh man, work's been crazy."

Ask him to watch his own child for four hours?

"I can't babysit tonight."

Sir, you cannot "babysit" someone genetically connected to you.

Their excuse playlist includes:
"Can we switch weekends?"

"Something came up."
"I didn't get that text."
"Traffic was bad."
"The court's unfair."
"My schedule is insane."
"I'll make it up next time." (He will not.)

## Top 10 Sentences You Only Hear From Part-Time Dads

The court's biased.
She's keeping the kid from me.
I'll make it next weekend.
Oh shoot, was that today?
My schedule is crazy.
He didn't act like this last time.
I'm doing my best. (He is not.)
I definitely sent the money.
Can we switch weekends?
I'm a great dad… when I have time.

This is why we can't have nice things.

## The Facebook Father

These dads don't parent.
They curate.

They vanish for weeks, then post a filtered photo with:
a heartfelt caption,
four emojis,
and zero involvement.

"Nothing more important than family!"

Meanwhile the full-time parent is reading that with a vein pulsing like Morse code.

Facebook Fathers:
argue in comment sections,
post conspiracy memes,
share motivational quotes,

…but call their own kid once a month:

"Sorry, I fell asleep."

If your relationship with your child exists mainly on Instagram, that's not parenting -

that's branding.

## The Holiday Hero

These dads operate exclusively on days with decorations.

Birthdays? Present.
Christmas? Present.
Halloween? Present.

But ask him for the kid's:
dentist,
teacher,
shoe size?

He'll guess like he's spinning a prize wheel.

Ask him about the custody clause regarding Christmas Eve at 4 p.m.?

Suddenly he's a constitutional scholar.

Holiday Heroes hide absence behind expensive gifts.

But kids want presence, not presents.

## The Part-Time Martyr

These dads believe the universe is unfair - specifically the parts involving consequences for their own behavior.

They love saying:
"She doesn't appreciate me."
"The courts screwed me."
"My schedule is insane."
"I'm doing everything I can."

Meanwhile the full-time parent is:
chef,
chauffeur,
tutor,
nurse,
referee,
therapist,
emotional crash pad.

They give 100%.
He performs at a confident 18% and wants a standing ovation.

This is why we can't have nice things.

# The Kid Who Summed Up Part-Time Parenting

I once saw a boy - maybe eight - sitting on a curb waiting for his dad.

His mom tried to soften the blow with cheerful lies:

"He's probably just running a little late!"

Thirty minutes passed.

Still no dad.

The kid didn't cry.
Didn't complain.
Didn't even look surprised.

He just shrugged and said:

"It's okay. I'm his Sunday kid."

That sentence should be handed out at custody hearings.

Kids understand absence long before they understand calendars.

# Kids Notice Everything

Kids don't care about:
excuses,
captions,
court filings,
gift bags.

They notice:
who shows up,
who remembers,
who listens,
who stays.

You can't fool a kid with a selfie.

They see the full story long before they can spell it.

This is why we can't have nice things.

## Supplemental Entries in the Deadbeat Dad Field Manual

### The Dad Who Thinks Parenting Has Seasons
"It's a rebuilding year."
"I'll get more time next season."
Sir, these are your children, not the Jacksonville Jaguars.

### The Shared Calendar Catastrophe
"I didn't see it!"
But you saw a meme from 2016 instantly.

### The Dad Who Treats Target as Parenting
Shows up with a $14 Nerf gun:
"See? I'm a good dad!"
Sir, that's retail, not fatherhood.

### The Magical Mystery Schedule
He's "busy" when responsibility appears.
Available instantly when his buddy texts:
"Bar tonight?"

**The Dad Who Overestimates His Importance**
"If the court wasn't biased, I'd have full custody."
And if I flap my arms hard enough, I'll fly.

## Types of Part-Time Dads

Disney Dad - chaos, cavities, and no bedtime.
Every-Other-Weekend…ish Dad - rarely where he's supposed to be.
Cash-App Father - sends $20 and calls it "support."
Courtroom Crusader - maximum effort only on court day.
Excuse Machine - new reason every week.
Holiday Hero - appears with gifts and vanishes in January.
Instagram Dad - posts more than he parents.
Victim Visionary - life is unfair; starring in his own documentary.
"I'll Make Up for It Later" Dad - spoiler: he won't.
Born-Again Dad - returns when the kid becomes fun.
The Pickup Phantom - always "five minutes away."
The Boundary Breaker - returns kids wired on sugar and adrenaline.
The Calendar Illiterate - can't read dates but can track fantasy football stats.
The Redemption Tour Dad - tries for two weeks, disappears for six months.

## Modern Society's Double Standard

Moms:
expected to do everything. Judged for everything.

Dads:
expected to do almost nothing. Praised for anything.

A dad buys groceries with a kid?
"Wow, what a great father!"

A mom does the same and the kid cries?
"Why can't she control her child?"

The bar for fatherhood is so low it's actively tunneling.

## Why This Chapter Matters

Part-time dads aren't just frustrating -
they reveal a deeper flaw in how our society treats parenting,
responsibility, and the expectations placed on mothers versus fathers.

This chapter matters because it exposes a truth people don't like saying
out loud:

Some men want the title of "Dad" without doing the work of being
one.

They want the photos,
the applause,
the holiday moments,
the curated social media image,
the identity of fatherhood -
without the daily effort that actually builds a child's life.

Meanwhile, the full-time parent - usually the mother - carries the
real weight:
the late nights,
the schoolwork,
the paperwork,
the doctor visits,
the emotional support,
the schedules,
the discipline,
the stability,

the invisible labor no one praises.

This chapter matters because it shines a light on a double standard so normalized most people don't even question it:

Moms are expected to be perfect.
Dads are applauded for showing up.

And kids?
Kids always know the truth.
They know who's present,
who's consistent,
who keeps their promises,
and who treats them like a weekend obligation.

Part-time dads don't just inconvenience the other parent -
they shape the stories kids tell themselves about worth, effort, and love.

Fatherhood isn't a hobby.
It isn't a seasonal role.
It isn't a photo opportunity.
It isn't content.

It's responsibility.
It's presence.
It's choosing your child every day - especially the hard ones.

And every time a dad treats parenting like optional overtime,
every time he posts instead of parents,
every time he shows up only when it's convenient,
we're reminded of the same painful truth:

This is why we can't have nice things.

# CHAPTER 20 - Holiday Creep: When Companies Celebrate Christmas in October

I swear, I can't buy Halloween candy anymore without tripping over a six-foot inflatable Santa that's already "doorbuster priced." And it's not just one store - every retailer in America is treating holidays like a competitive speedrun.

Halloween? Too old.
Thanksgiving? Too boring.
Christmas? RELEASE IT IMMEDIATELY.

Companies expect us to be spooky, grateful, patriotic, romantic, and jolly - all while still paying off last year's holiday debt. Stores treat holidays the way fast-food chains treat combo meals: if they could shove three more in there, they would.

Holiday creep is America's way of saying:

"Don't enjoy the moment - BUY THE NEXT ONE."

And let's be honest:

This is why we can't have nice things.

## Christmas in October... Sometimes September

Remember when Christmas didn't start until after Thanksgiving?

Pepperidge Farm remembers.
Corporations do not.

Now Christmas starts whenever a retailer needs a quarterly bump - usually somewhere between "kids are still swimming" and "you haven't put away your summer shorts yet?".

You walk into Target in early October expecting pumpkins...
Instead, you walk into a fake tree farm.
Left: witches and skeletons
Right: Santa and reindeer
Aisle center: peppermint-flavored everything brawling with pumpkin spice in a seasonal turf war

The day Christmas officially lost its mind was the day a store played Jingle Bells before kids had even finished trick-or-treating.

Nothing says spooky season like hearing Mariah Carey clearing her throat in late September.

## Thanksgiving: The Forgotten Middle Child

Thanksgiving is the overlooked middle child of American holidays.
Halloween gets costumes, candy, parties.
Christmas gets nostalgia, movies, sales, decorations, dominance.
Thanksgiving gets... one sad turkey inflatable and a gravy packet.

Retailers treat Thanksgiving like a brief commercial break between:

"Spooky Stuff We Can Mark Up"
and
"Holiday Crap We Can Sell for 90 Days Straight."

The day after Halloween, stores start screaming:

"ONLY 54 DAYS UNTIL CHRISTMAS!"

Meanwhile Thanksgiving is in the corner mumbling, "I exist…"

Black Friday is so aggressive it's basically eating Thanksgiving from the inside. Some places don't even pretend anymore - the Black Friday ads start before the mashed potatoes hit the table.

If November 1st doesn't feel like a hostage situation, you haven't been in a mall lately.

Thanksgiving isn't even a holiday anymore - it's a speed bump between two marketing campaigns.

## The Corporate Motivation: Panic and Profit

Why do companies do this?

One word: money.
Two words: desperate money.

Retailers weaponize:
fake scarcity,
manufactured urgency,
countdown timers,
"limited-time offers,"
"buy now before it's gone!,"

…for items that will be sitting on clearance in mid-January next to discounted wrapping paper and a crushed snowman.

Holiday creep is just capitalism juggling anxiety and glitter:

Decorations → candy → leftover decorations → clearance → repeat.

It's not holiday spirit - it's holiday desperation with LED lights.

## Holiday Identity Crisis

No holiday is safe anymore.
Valentine's Day shows up January 2,
Easter baskets hop into stores in February,
Fourth of July merch hits in late April.

You go to Home Depot for a wrench and get ambushed by:
Valentine hearts,
pastel bunnies,
patriotic pinwheels,
fall décor,
and a 10-foot snowman who definitely knows your credit score.

And somehow, none of this helps you find the damn wrench.

You walk out without the wrench, but with a full-blown seasonal identity crisis.

It's always the next holiday.
Never the one we're actually in.

## The Three-Holiday Shopping Trip

I once went to the store for one thing: a bag of Halloween candy.

I walk in - immediately smacked in the face by Christmas. Full trees, wreaths, animatronic Santa gyrating whenever someone walks by.

Annoying, but fine.

I head toward the candy aisle. Halloween has been shoved into three sad endcaps like seasonal leftovers that missed the eviction notice.

Then I turn a corner and nearly run into a giant inflatable turkey holding a sign that says:

"IT'S ALMOST THANKSGIVING!"

It was October 8.

At the checkout, there's a "Valentine's Day Preview" display:
pink teddy bears,
chocolate roses,
heart-shaped everything.

In October.
Under canned Christmas music.

So there I am holding:
Halloween candy,
surrounded by Thanksgiving turkeys,
under a Valentine's banner,
while Santa croons overhead.

My brain short-circuited. Should I carve a pumpkin? Baste a turkey? Wrap a gift? Propose?

All I wanted was candy.

As I walked out, an employee cheerfully said:

"Come back next week, Easter stuff goes out!"

And that was the moment I knew:

This is why we can't have nice things.

## The Emotional Whiplash

Holiday creep isn't just annoying - it's exhausting.

Humans were not designed to be in "holiday mode" for three consecutive months. But corporations don't care.
Be spooky!
Be grateful!
Be joyful!
Be generous!
Be romantic!
Spend early!
Spend often!

By December 1, you're burnt out and still have weeks left of mandatory cheer.

Kids walk into stores in October and see:
skeletons,
pumpkins,
turkeys,
elves,
nativity scenes,
giant inflatable polar bears.

All in one aisle.

Of course they're confused. Retail turned childhood into a seasonal glitch.

## When Holidays Overlap Like a Bad Venn Diagram

We've hit the point where holidays are literally sharing shelf space:

Santa in a witch hat,
skeletons posed next to nativity scenes,
pumpkins beside candy canes,
ghosts holding menorahs.

Stores forget to take things down so we get Franken-holidays nobody asked for.

I once saw a chocolate bunny sitting proudly in a Fourth of July display.

Pure chaos.

## Why Holiday Creep Pisses Me Off

Holiday creep ruins the whole point of holidays.

They're supposed to:
mean something,
break up the year,
create special moments,
give us something to look forward to.

Now they're just:

"Q4 revenue opportunities."

Seeing Christmas trees in September feels like the calendar has suffered a nervous breakdown.

We're stuck in a nonstop loop:

Halloween → Christmas → Valentine's Day → Easter → Patriotic Stuff → Pumpkin Spice → repeat.

No pause.
No breathing room.
No "right now."

And that?

This is why we can't have nice things.

## The Good Old Days (Yes, I'm Going There)

I remember when:
stores didn't decorate for Christmas until after Thanksgiving,
holidays stayed roughly in their lanes,
Christmas started in December, not Labor Day weekend,
pumpkin spice didn't invade August.

Was it perfect? No.
Was it saner? Absolutely.

We had one holiday at a time like civilized human beings, not six stacked on top of each other in a retail Jenga tower.

## Why This Chapter Matters

Holiday creep isn't just annoying - it's a symptom of something bigger, louder, and more exhausting happening in modern life.

This chapter matters because it reveals how companies have turned time itself into a product.
We don't get seasons anymore.
We don't get moments.
We don't even get breathing room.

We get a nonstop conveyor belt of:

BUY THIS.
BE FESTIVE.
HURRY UP.
YOU'RE LATE FOR THE NEXT HOLIDAY.

Retail has blurred the calendar so badly that even kids don't know what season they're in. When a five-year-old sees Santa, a skeleton, a turkey, and a pastel bunny in the same aisle, it's not whimsy - it's confusion disguised as cheer.

Holiday creep trains us to skip the present and sprint toward what's next.
It turns joy into urgency.
Tradition into marketing.
Nostalgia into inventory.

And beneath all the glitter and countdown timers is a deeper loss:
We're forgetting how to be present.
How to enjoy one thing at a time.
How to take a breath before the next wave of "limited-time offers."

Holidays used to anchor the year.
Now they blur it.

This chapter matters because it reminds us that meaning requires space - and corporations sure as hell aren't giving it to us.

And every time Christmas shows up before the leaves even change, every time stores shove six holidays into one aisle, every time a season gets rushed, stretched, and monetized out of recognition, we're reminded of the truth:

This is why we can't have nice things.

# CHAPTER 21 - Adults Who Shouldn't Be Adults

There are people walking around this world - fully grown, tax-paying, licensed to drive - who absolutely should not be left unsupervised.

I don't think some folks "grew into" adulthood. I think one day they just woke up with:
a driver's license,
a credit score,
a Netflix subscription,

...and immediately started misusing all three.

We all know them.
We all work with them.
Some of us are related to them.

These are the grown humans who:
panic at a simple form,
think "deductible" is a personal insult,
still survive on ramen at 42,
burn water,
treat the Wi-Fi going out like an extinction-level event.

And collectively?

This is why we can't have nice things.

# The Form-Filling Disaster

Nobody likes paperwork.
But there's a difference between "ugh, forms" and "emotionally shattered by 'Print Clearly.'"

These adults stare at basic forms like they're carved in ancient runes.

Name.
Address.
Date.
Signature.

Their brain hits airplane mode.

They ask:
"Do I put today's date or my birthday?"
"Is ZIP code required?"
"Wait… what's my email again?"

How do you forget your email?
It's literally your name plus a number you made up in 2009.

You tell them "Sign here" and they print their name.
You tell them "Print here" and they sign in cursive.
And no matter what… they ALWAYS write in the section that clearly says:

DO NOT WRITE BELOW THIS LINE.

These people can vote. And drive.

This is why we can't have nice things.

## Adults Who Don't Understand Insurance

Nothing exposes a barely-functional adult faster than insurance.

Health. Car. Renters. Dental. Doesn't matter - they understand none of it.

They ask:
"What's a deductible?"
"Why do I pay premiums and copays?"
"If I have insurance, why do I still pay anything?"

They act like you personally designed the U.S. healthcare system.

They treat insurance like astrology - confusing, mystical, and somehow always retrograde when they need it.

They always buy the plan called something like:

"Economy Bronze Saver Lite Basic Mini Coverage Option"

...and are SHOCKED when it covers absolutely nothing.

Their cycle:
Pick the cheapest plan,
Need something,
Yell at everyone,
Repeat.

This is why we can't have nice things.

## Zero Life Skills: The Walking "How?"

Some adults barely qualify as domesticated.

They can't:
cook,
budget,
clean,
grocery shop without a group text.

Ask them to boil pasta and you get:
"How much water?"
"How hot?"
"Do I stir it?"
"Do I need a pot?"

Yes.
You need a pot.
We live in a society.

Hand them a recipe and they look at it like it's an encrypted message from NASA.

Their diet is:
pizza rolls,
ramen,
takeout,
regret.

They've never used an iron.
They think trash day is "flexible."
Their laundry hamper is a myth - it's just the floor.

Life skills?
None.

## Ramen as a Personality

There's enjoying ramen…

And then there's being 42 and treating it like it's a medical plan.

They say stuff like:

"I'm actually a pretty good cook - I make amazing ramen."

No, you don't.
You added cheese and hot sauce.

If your stove has only ever seen:
ramen,
frozen pizza,
scented candles…

…then yes - you are part of the problem.

This is why we can't have nice things.

## Adults Who Burn Water

We need to talk about people who set off the smoke alarm boiling water.

Not cooking a full meal.
Not frying.
Not baking.

Boiling.
Water.

How do you burn water?

These are the same people who:
microwave aluminum foil,
put plastic in the oven,

melt Tupperware like performance art.

Every kitchen they enter becomes a future insurance claim.

## Wi-Fi Outage = Societal Collapse

No meltdown compares to a grown adult losing Wi-Fi.

The second the signal drops, they become pioneers on the Oregon Trail:
unplugging the router,
turning their phone sideways like that helps,
standing on chairs for "better reception,"
rebooting 14 times,
calling tech support after 90 seconds of suffering.

"My Netflix froze!"
"My TikTok won't load!"
"What am I supposed to DO?"

You could:
read,
sit,
think,
go outside,
touch an actual physical object.

Suggest any of this and they react like you've proposed medieval torture.

They look at you like you suggested witchcraft.

The moment their digital leash snaps, all life skills vanish.

This is why we can't have nice things.

# The Adult Child Crisis

We ALL know at least one person who:
still writes checks at the grocery store,
doesn't know their bank login,
thinks APR is a sports stat,
finds out their license is expired at the airport,
doesn't know how to refill windshield wiper fluid,
owns three dead plants,
calls their parents to make doctor's appointments,
still doesn't understand taxes after 20 years of filing them.

These people operate motor vehicles daily.
It's a miracle the country still functions.

We're one missed reminder away from these people becoming a true-crime documentary.

# Types of Adults Who Shouldn't Be Adults

### The "I Don't Know How to Fill Out a Form" Adult
Lines + words = emotional shutdown.

### The "What's a Deductible?" Adult
Asks this every year like it's brand new information.

### The Microwave Chef
Cooks exclusively by beep and steam.

### The Boiling Water Arsonist
A fire hazard with a saucepan.

### The Ramen Connoisseur
Adds cheese and thinks it's "elevated."

**The Wi-Fi Collapse Survivor**
Loses all hope when the little bars disappear.

**The Phone-Call Avoider**
Would rather endure tooth pain than call the dentist.

**The "I'll Google It Later" Adult**
Spoiler: they will not.

**The Tool-Impaired DIY Warrior**
Can't tell a wrench from a ritual object.

**The Perpetual Crisis Generator**
Every day is a preventable emergency.

**The Expired-Document Champion**
Only discovers problems at TSA.

**The Domestic Disaster**
Laundry? Dishes? Never heard of her.
Believes 'deep cleaning' means lighting a candle.

**The "I'll Do It Tomorrow" Adult**
Tomorrow = never.

**The Bank-Account Acrobat**
Budgets via overdraft.

**The "I Don't Know How Cars Work" Driver**
Owns one. Understands none.

**The Tech Fossil**
Fifteen pending updates. Proud of it.

**The Plant Serial Killer**
Kills succulents. SUCCULENTS.

**The Confused Shopper**
Goes in for milk. Leaves with candles and no milk.

## Why These Adults Piss Me Off

Nobody needs to know everything.

But basic functioning should not be optional downloadable content.

Being an adult means:
learning,
adapting,
paying attention,
handling minor tasks without a meltdown,
surviving inconvenience without becoming a cautionary tale.

Too many people skipped that part and went straight to:

"Complain loudly and hope someone fixes it."

And this?

This is why we can't have nice things.

## Why This Chapter Matters

Adulthood isn't just a legal status -
it's a collection of responsibilities that keep society from collapsing into pure chaos.

When grown adults can't:
fill out basic forms,
manage simple tasks,
understand their own insurance,

or survive a brief inconvenience without melting down,
it doesn't just affect them.

It affects everyone around them.

This chapter matters because it exposes a truth most people quietly tolerate every day:

Too many adults are outsourcing their adulthood.

They're handing off:
the mental load,
the problem-solving,
the basic functioning,
to whoever is closest and more competent.

And that burden almost always falls on:
partners,
coworkers,
friends,
parents,
anyone unlucky enough to be within earshot during a Wi-Fi outage.

We're not talking about people facing real barriers or genuine hardship.
We're talking about adults who never developed the skills,
the effort,
or the resilience,
needed to operate as actual grown-ups -
because someone else has always handled it for them.

And when basic adult functioning becomes optional, it doesn't just inconvenience others…

It creates a society where:
incompetence is normalized,

helplessness is rewarded,
responsibility is avoided,
and the people who *do* their part end up carrying the weight for everyone who doesn't.

Kids notice it.
Coworkers absorb it.
Partners burn out from it.
Systems strain under it.

Adulthood only works when adults collectively act like adults.

Because every time someone treats boiling pasta like rocket science,
every time a grown human cries over a deductible,
every time a preventable crisis becomes someone else's emergency,
we're reminded again:

This is why we can't have nice things.

# CHAPTER 22 - Influencers: The New Used-Car Salesmen

Once upon a time, the sleaziest salesmen in America wore plaid suits, slicked-back hair, and sold you a car that would explode within 40 miles.

Now?

They hold ring lights, drink iced coffee like it's a personality trait, and shout motivational nonsense into a camera.

Welcome to the age of influencers - the modern used-car salesmen.

Same energy.
New packaging.

And honestly?

This is why we can't have nice things.

## Fake Expertise: Everyone's a Guru Now

Influencers have made expertise completely meaningless.

You used to need:
credentials,
education,
experience,
or at least one functioning brain cell,

...before telling people how to live their lives.

Now all you need is:
a ring light,
good lighting,
three buzzwords,
and an audience of people who stopped thinking in 2015.

Suddenly, someone who hasn't opened a book since high school is a:
financial coach,
nutrition expert,
mental health advocate,
skincare specialist,
relationship strategist,
fitness guru,
success mentor,
productivity consultant,
"energy healer."

They're one quote away from selling a $399 "masterclass" on how to unlock your inner sparkle.

They'll say things like:

"Here's the #1 secret to wealth: BELIEVE IT!"

Oh, thank God.
For a second I thought the answer might be something complicated like... having money.

## Fake Personalities: Mascots of Nothingness

Influencers have perfected the art of being aggressively upbeat for absolutely no reason.

They pop onto your screen at 6 a.m. screaming:

"GOOD MORNING BESTIESSSS!!! YOU DESERVE JOY!!!!"

I'm sorry:
Who are you yelling at?
Why are you yelling?
And why does your enthusiasm feel like a threat?

Their personalities are clearly factory-made - same cadence, same catchphrases, same "unhinged but quirky" energy. They're basically Disney Channel hosts with promo codes.

Meet them in real life and they're quiet, awkward, and shaped like a damp paper towel.

But online?

They're the human version of an energy drink.

It's all fake. It has to be.

No one is that excited about moisturizer.

## Fake Lives: The Carefully Edited Fantasy

Influencers don't have lives.
They have highlight reels.

Perfect homes.
Perfect lighting.
Perfect bodies.
Perfect relationships.

All curated to make you feel like you're failing.

Behind the scenes?
Their kitchen smells like old takeout and regret.
Their relationships are imploding in real time.
Their money comes from pretending they have more money.
Their mental health is held together with duct tape and affirmations.

Their homes look minimalist because everything they own is shoved just outside the camera frame.

All so they can sell you the illusion that they "have it all figured out."

Spoiler: no one has it figured out.
Especially not someone whose entire identity fits into a 30-second TikTok.

## Endless Sponsorships: Everything Costs $39.99

Influencers will swear something "changed their life" -
if the check clears first.

You click on a video:

"Here's how I stay productive every morning!"

Two seconds later:

"This video is sponsored by Magic Vitamin Powder™ - clinically proven to do absolutely nothing!"

They'll push:
supplements,
apps,
clothes,

diet programs,
skincare routines,
hair gummies,
meditation pillows,
mystery powders...

...all with the authenticity of someone reading cue cards at gunpoint.

They always swear:

"I only partner with brands I truly believe in."

Buddy.

You have "truly believed in" 47 brands this month.

At this point, their bloodstream is 30% affiliate links.

It's like watching QVC, but with filters and denial.

## "Use My Promo Code!" Culture

Influencers LOVE giving out promo codes.

Promo codes are:
currency,
validation,
proof of existence.

"Use my code JESSICA10!"
"Use my code FITDAD20!"
"Use my code GIRLBOSS15 for 15% off your emotional support water bottle!"

Some try to disguise it:

"This isn't sponsored, I just REALLY love this product, but if you want to support me you can click the affiliate link in my bio!"

That's like saying:

"This isn't a robbery, I just REALLY love your wallet, but if you want to support me, hand it over."

Everything is a pyramid scheme disguised as self-care.

## People Who Shout Inspiration at a Ring Light

Then we have the "motivators" - the ones who scream encouragement at you like caffeinated cult leaders.

Pointing at the camera:

"YOU need to STOP making excuses!"
"YOU need to TAKE CONTROL of your life!"
"YOU need to stop letting fear hold you back!"

Sir, you are filming this in your bathroom.
Calm down.

It always crescendos into:

"IF I CAN DO IT, YOU CAN DO IT!"

Okay, but... what exactly did you do?

Because from where I'm sitting, all you've done is yell for 60 seconds and monetize it.

Real motivation looks like actual effort, not someone screaming at strangers between brand deals.

## The Authenticity Illusion

Influencers talk about "being real" more than anyone else on the planet.

They'll post:

"Just keeping it honest with you guys. Today was hard."

Attached to:
a perfectly edited black-and-white photo,
soft focus,
immaculate lighting,
a caption that ends with a promo link.

Authenticity isn't content.
Authenticity is… being authentic.

If your "raw, unfiltered moment" took 37 takes and a Lightroom preset, it's not raw. It's marketing.

## The Parasocial Circus

People form emotional bonds with influencers like they're long-distance friends.

"She's so relatable."
"He's just like us!"
"I feel like I really know them!"

No, you don't.

You know the character they play for you.

If your relationship with someone exists only through a screen, that isn't friendship. That's customer loyalty.

You're not their friend - you're their metrics.

## The Collapse of Expertise

Remember when:
scientists talked about science,
doctors talked about medicine,
chefs talked about food,
mechanics talked about cars?

Now influencers do all of that. Poorly.
And people listen.

We now have:
beauty gurus diagnosing medical issues,
lifestyle influencers giving financial advice,
gym bros acting like licensed therapists,
food bloggers teaching food safety while stroking raw chicken and strawberries in the same frame.

We stopped valuing actual experts and replaced them with people who speak confidently while mispronouncing basic words.

Confidence has officially replaced competence - and apparently that's all it takes now.

This is not a metaphor.

This is literally why we can't have nice things.

# Why Influencers Piss Me Off

Influencing isn't inherently evil.

What's rotten is:
fake expertise,
filtered personalities,
highlight-reel lives,
manipulative marketing,
constant monetization.

They've turned the internet into a digital used-car lot:

"THIS PRODUCT WILL CHANGE YOUR LIFE!"
"THE ONE SECRET YOUR DOCTOR WON'T TELL YOU!"
"BUY THIS OR YOU'LL DIE ALONE!"

Influencers are everywhere, selling everything, pretending to know everything.

And society eats it up with a ring-light spoon.

We are being sold to 24/7, and the worst part?
A lot of people don't even notice.

# Why This Chapter Matters

Influencers aren't just irritating -
they expose a deeper problem with how we decide who deserves our attention.

This chapter matters because it reveals a truth most people quietly ignore:

Too many of us are confusing confidence with competence.

Influencers have made it easy to mistake:
polish for expertise,
enthusiasm for credibility,
aesthetic for authenticity,
a ring light for actual qualifications.

And when charisma beats knowledge, the consequences aren't just annoying - they're real.

Because the louder someone is online, the more we treat them like authorities on:
health,
money,
relationships,
nutrition,
mental well-being,
lifestyle choices,

...despite the fact that many of them have no training, no background, and no idea what they're talking about.

Meanwhile, the people who *should* be guiding these conversations - the doctors, the scientists, the financial experts, the teachers - get drowned out by someone who opens every video screaming:

"HEYYY BESTIESSS!!!"

Influencers also distort reality itself.
They sell highlight reels as truth.
They sell perfection as normal.
They sell fantasy as fact.
They sell insecurity as opportunity.

And every time someone buys into a curated life built on:
filters,

sponsorships,
affiliate links,
manufactured relatability,
and strategic vulnerability…

…the line between genuine advice and monetized manipulation gets thinner.

This chapter matters because it calls out the shift happening right under our noses:

We've stopped valuing substance.
We've started rewarding spectacle.

Expertise used to matter.
Now it's whoever can yell the loudest into a front-facing camera.

And every time fake "gurus" replace real knowledge, every time people fall for curated authenticity, every time a promo code masquerades as wisdom, we're reminded - again and again:

This is why we can't have nice things.

# CHAPTER 23 - People Who Overshare on Social Media

Some people treat Facebook like a diary, Instagram like a confessional, TikTok like a therapist, and Snapchat like a burner phone for bad decisions.

These are the humans who believe the entire internet needs to know:
what they ate,
how they slept,
what argument they had,
what medical condition they might have,
which coworker wronged them,
what their ex did in 2014,
and how "some people need to stay in their lane."

Oversharers.
Chronic posters.
The human equivalent of a 24-hour news cycle nobody requested.

And of course:

This is why we can't have nice things.

## The Meal-By-Meal Documentarians

Every meal.
EVERY. SINGLE. MEAL.

Breakfast:

"Eggs and toast with a side of positivity!"

Lunch:

"Fueling my grind! #SaladLife"

Dinner:
A blurry photo of beige pasta on a paper plate:

"Made this masterpiece tonight"

Masterpiece?
It looks like a crime scene at Olive Garden.

These are the same people who take 14 photos of their latte art like they're applying for a museum grant.

You know what most people call photographing every meal?

A cry for help.

And not even a creative one - it's the emotional equivalent of a Post-It note.

## The Relationship Broadcast Network

Oversharers do not experience romance quietly.

They treat every breakup, makeup, argument, and jealousy spiral like a serialized drama.

**Monday:**
"My ride-or-die"

**Tuesday:**
"Some people are fake."

**Wednesday:**
"I deserve better."

**Thursday:**
Status: deleted.

**Friday:**
"He's my everything!"

Nobody asked.
Nobody needed play-by-play coverage.

Stop dragging the entire internet into your bargain-bin soap opera.

## Medical Updates Nobody Asked For

There's a special breed of oversharer who treats Facebook like a HIPAA-free medical memoir.

"My back hurts again keep me in your prayers!"

"My stomach is acting up… does anyone know what this rash is?"

"Just got out of the ER… long story."

Then the photos start:
swollen limbs,
stitched wounds,
oozing rashes,
X-rays they don't understand.

No warning. No blur. Just raw, high-definition infection.

You can feel your immune system shutting down just scrolling past it.

## Vaguebooking: The Art of Suggestive Melodrama

Vaguebookers are the Shakespeare of attention-seeking.

Posts like:
"I'm done."
"You know who you are."
"Some people... WOW."
"Pray for me."
"It's always the ones you trust."

No context. Just bait.

Within minutes:
"What happened???"
"DM me now!"
"Are you okay??"

Exactly the reaction they wanted.

It's not a cry for help.
It's a fishing trip.

## Trauma Dumpers

Trauma dumpers will unload decades of emotional baggage in the comments of a cheesecake recipe.

You're watching:

"How to make creamy chicken pasta!"

Then, suddenly:

"When I was seven my uncle stole $40 from me and I've never trusted anyone since."

Ma'am.
This is Alfredo.

Seek therapy. Not the comment section.

Trauma dumping is emotional littering.
Stop throwing your problems onto the digital sidewalk.

And just when you think you've seen the peak of oversharing...

## The Overshare That Broke My Brain

I was scrolling Facebook - AKA the digital nursing home - and saw a post from a woman I barely knew in high school. We're talking "shared a lab table once" level acquaintance.

Her post starts:

"Please respect my privacy during this difficult time."

Immediately followed by a multi-paragraph confession explaining everything in graphic detail.

It begins mild:

"My husband and I are going through some issues..."

Then escalates:

"…because he hasn't touched me in three months and I think it's because he's addicted to Fortnite."

Ma'am.
What.

She includes:
screenshots of their text fight,
timestamps,
his misspelled insults,
her dramatic monologues,
a photo of the casserole she made "to save the marriage."

Then she posts A POLL:

"Do you guys think he's cheating or just emotionally constipated?"
A) Cheating
B) Constipated
C) Both

Two hundred people voted.

Then the husband storms into the comments:

"Why are you posting this on Facebook? Also the casserole sucked."

I almost called 911 from secondhand embarrassment.

By the end:
people were taking sides,
some recommended therapy,
some recommended divorce,
at least three older ladies were praying in the comments.

Then she went live.

Sobbing.
Mascara streaks.
Dog barking.
Chaos.

At this point I had to step away from my phone, take a breath, and remind myself -

This is why we can't have nice things.

## Types of Oversharers

### The Medical Exhibit
Posts every bruise, bump, rash, and medical mystery in 4K.

### The Emotional Arsonist
Drops vague cries for attention then disappears for 48 hours.

### The Livestream Lunatic
Goes live during arguments, errands, dental cleanings, and emotional breakdowns.

### The Motivational Screamer
Posts sunrise speeches while their personal life is in structural collapse.

### The Relationship Historian
Documents every text, conflict, breakup, reconciliation, and sub-breakup.

### The Kitchen Cryptid
Posts unseasoned beige meals and calls it "chef life."

# The Professional Life Recorders

Some people don't actually experience life - they just film it.
Baby's first steps? Record.
Argument in public? Record.
Grandma blowing out candles? Record.
Car accident? Record.

Funeral?
You know at least one person thought about it.

They don't live in the moment.
They live next to the moment while shouting, "Wait, do it again for the video!"

"If I didn't post it, did it even happen?"

Yes.
Life existed before your Instagram story.

# The Daily Inspiration Yellers

These are the people who post motivational speeches at ungodly hours:

"RISE AND GRIND!"
"You ARE worthy!"
"Today is YOUR day!"

Okay, Dollar Store Tony Robbins.
It's 4:17 a.m.

Meanwhile, their personal life resembles a dumpster fire behind a Waffle House.

Crazy idea:

Try fixing your life before narrating everyone else's.

## The Family Oversharers

Some parents treat their kids like content:
every recital,
every meltdown,
every medical issue,
every embarrassing moment,
every tantrum filmed and posted for "relatable" likes.

Those kids are going to grow up, Google themselves, and discover their entire childhood archived like a public case study in bad judgment.

Not every moment has to be captured.
Some of them are just… parenting.

## Some People Would Livestream Their Own Arrest

You know I'm right.

A certain kind of oversharer would get handcuffed and still look straight at the camera:

"Hey guys, today got CRAZY I was just out here living my truth and - officer, say hi to the vlog!"

At that point it's not oversharing.
It's pathology.

# Why Oversharers Piss Me Off

Not everything needs to be:
posted,
shared,
documented,
hashtagged,
streamed,
discussed with distant cousins and ex-coworkers.

Oversharing doesn't create connection.
It creates digital noise.

We do not need:
your medical records,
your relationship meltdowns,
your inspirational monologues,
your 37 blurry photos of spaghetti.

The constant feed of personal chaos clogs the internet like emotional hair in the shower drain.

And truly?

This is why we can't have nice things.

# Why This Chapter Matters

Oversharing online isn't just annoying -
it reveals how badly we've blurred the line between private life and public spectacle.

This chapter matters because it pulls the curtain back on something most of us quietly tolerate:

People broadcasting every emotion, every argument, every rash, every crisis -
not to connect,
not to heal,
but to *perform*.

And when everything becomes content,
nothing stays meaningful.

Oversharing dumps the emotional labor onto:
friends,
coworkers,
strangers online,
anyone scrolling within range.

It turns real problems into entertainment.
It turns boundaries into punchlines.
It turns the internet into a landfill of other people's unresolved issues.

This chapter matters because it asks a simple question:

If everything is shared, what's left that's actually yours?

Healthy relationships - real ones - require privacy, trust, boundaries, and actual conversation, not a livestreamed meltdown or a Facebook poll about your marriage.

Oversharing doesn't create community.
It creates noise.
It creates burnout.
It creates an internet where nobody remembers what normal looks like.

And every time someone posts their medical chart, their breakup transcript, or their child's worst moment for likes?

We're reminded once again:

This is why we can't have nice things.

# CHAPTER 24 - Why Customer Loyalty Programs Are Scams

Somewhere along the way, companies decided that giving you good service and fair prices wasn't enough. That would've been far too reasonable. Too simple. Too... honest.
Instead, they invented a system that looks like a reward but behaves like a trap:

Customer loyalty programs.

A corporate carnival game where the prizes suck, the rules keep changing, and the house wins every time. These programs are the modern equivalent of dangling shiny objects in front of a raccoon - and we, the raccoons, fall for it every damn time.

And honestly?

This is why we can't have nice things.

## Points That Expire Like Spoiled Milk

You earn points for spending money.
You save those points.
You fantasize about the "reward" you'll finally redeem someday.

Then - right when you're close - your app delivers the gut punch:

"Your points have expired!"

Expired?

They're not bananas.
They don't mold.
They are imaginary numbers in a server somewhere.

Companies invent points... then decide the points they invented go stale if you don't worship them fast enough. Points don't expire. Companies just get exhausted pretending they owe you anything.

## Reward Tiers: The Corporate Pyramid Scheme

Every loyalty program comes with tiers - Bronze, Silver, Gold, Platinum, Diamond, Obsidian, Supreme Emperor of Latte Buyers - each one slightly more ridiculous than the last.

Every tier promises "exclusive perks," but only after you spend enough money to qualify for a small business loan.

You want the good rewards?
Simple: just spend $2,000 a year on coffee you don't even like.

And the "reward" you unlock?
A slightly less miserable version of what you should've received as a basic human right.

## Loyalty Math That Should Be Illegal

Nothing reveals the stupidity of loyalty programs like coffee shop math.

Buy a $6 latte → earn .5 points.
Need 500 points for a free drink.
Do the math.

You must spend enough money to finance a medium-sized wedding for a "free" iced coffee that cost them fourteen cents to make.

And right when you get close, they hit you with the mandatory disappointment:

"Starting next month, free drinks now require 750 points!"

Perfect.
Now you need to take out a second mortgage for a cold brew.

And every time a company pretends this is a "reward," we're reminded yet again:

This is why we can't have nice things.

## The App They Swear You "Need"

Every store now wants you to download their app - not for convenience, not for service, but because they want to track you like a tagged wildlife project.

They want to know:
how often you buy snacks,
which impulse purchases defeat you,
what coupons seduce you,
how to manipulate you better next time.

You try to buy a bag of chips and the cashier hits you with:

"Do you have our app? You could save $0.14!"

I'm not giving you my email, phone number, and soul for a discount that wouldn't even buy a single peanut.

## Stores Pretending They're Doing You a Favor

"Join our loyalty program!"
"Be part of our family!"
"Unlock exclusive savings!"

If your "family" demands my birthday, phone number, mailing address, and DNA sample before selling me detergent, I'm not joining a loyalty program - I'm joining a cult with coupons.

## The Free Muffin That Wasn't

I once tried redeeming a "FREE MUFFIN!" reward from a coffee shop.

I show the cashier my app.

She scans it, squints, and says:

"Oh... this only applies to *select* muffins."

I ask, "Which muffins are select?"

She gestures at an empty tray like she's unveiling a magic trick.

"We're out of those."

Then she says I can get $0.35 off a full-priced muffin instead.

At that point, I didn't want a muffin - I wanted justice.

This alone could have carried the thesis of the chapter:

This is why we can't have nice things.

## The Illusion of Savings

Stores love guilt-tripping you with receipts that say:

"You saved $38.21 today!"

No, I didn't.
You inflated the price, fake-discounted it, and tried to gaslight me into gratitude.

If you want me to save money, here's a revolutionary idea:

Just lower the price.

## The Scam Is the System

Customer loyalty programs are engineered to:
get you hooked on dopamine,
keep you buying what you don't need,
track your behavior,
guilt you into "loyalty,"
distract you from the price hikes,
make you believe you're earning something.

It's the adult version of Chuck E. Cheese:

Spend $200 to win a pencil eraser.

And the eraser doesn't even work - it just smears the mistake around like a metaphor.

# Types of Loyalty Scams (A Corporate Field Guide)

**Expiring Points**
Poof - gone. Like they were never real. Because they weren't.

**Impossible Tier Levels**
Earn elite status by spending enough to buy a used car.

**App-Only Discounts**
Give us your data and we'll give you a coupon worth spare change.

**Inflated Price Discounts**
Raise prices → "discount" the hike → profit.

**The Free Item That Isn't Free**
Buy 4 things you don't want to earn 1 thing you barely want.

**Receipt Surveys for 10 Points**
Thirty minutes of your life for a reward worth half a stale cookie.

**Automatic Enrollment**
One purchase = seven emails a day until you die.

**Phone Number Loyalty Tracking**
Congratulations, you're now a corporate lab rat.

**Rules Changing Monthly**
Always in the company's favor. Never in yours.

**"You Have Rewards!" (That You Can't Use)**
Your reward is a coupon for something you'd never buy, valid only between 2-3 a.m. during a lunar eclipse.

# Why Loyalty Programs Piss Me Off

Because loyalty should be earned, not gamified.

Good business is simple:
fair prices,
good products,
good service.

But companies today want:
your money,
your data,
your habits,
your trust,
your patterns,
your loyalty.

All in exchange for fake digital currency that evaporates whenever convenient.

This is why we can't have nice things.

# Why This Chapter Matters

Customer loyalty programs aren't harmless.
They're not cute.
They're not "fun perks" or "little bonuses."

They're corporate psychology experiments disguised as rewards.

This chapter matters because it exposes the truth companies don't want you to think about:

Loyalty programs are designed to manipulate your behavior, not reward it.

They turn:
spending into a game,
tracking into a normal expectation,
data extraction into a "perk,"
and imaginary points into a substitute for fair pricing.

And while companies pretend they're "giving" you something, what they're actually taking is far more valuable:
your habits,
your spending patterns,
your attention,
your personal information,
your sense of what a reasonable price even is.

Points don't make things cheaper -
they make you numb to how expensive everything became.

Loyalty programs don't build loyalty -
they build dependency.

They teach people to chase:
tiers,
badges,
status labels,
small perks,
and discounts that only exist because prices were inflated in the first place.

Meanwhile, companies quietly move the goalposts:
points expire,
rewards change,
tiers get harder to reach,
benefits shrink,
and the system resets right when you're close to earning something.

This chapter matters because it calls out the illusion:

You're working for rewards that were never designed for you to actually reach.

It's the adult version of collecting arcade tickets -
and the prize is always disappointing.

And every time a company asks for your data, every time a cashier pushes an app, every time points evaporate overnight like imaginary smoke, we're reminded - yet again:

This is why we can't have nice things.

# CHAPTER 25 - Why Every Company Wants Me to Take a Damn Survey

At some point, every company in America collectively decided they were emotionally fragile. You can't buy anything - anything - without being stalked for feedback like you just ended a messy relationship.

You buy socks, walk to your car, and suddenly your phone vibrates like you owe someone child support.

"How did we do?"
"Rate your experience!"
"Take our survey - it'll only take 5 minutes!"

Five minutes?
Buddy, I bought socks. I'm not critiquing a Broadway performance.

And once again:

This is why we can't have nice things.

## Receipts: The Survey Scroll of Doom

Receipts used to be one line and a total. Now they're a dissertation.

Cashiers circle the survey section dramatically, like they're handing you a treasure map to financial salvation:

"You could win $500!"

No, I can't.
Nobody wins.
The prize is a myth corporations invented to justify emotional harassment.

## The Multi-Channel Attack

Before you reach your car:
1 email,
1 text,
1 push notification,
and sometimes a second survey reminding you you've ignored the first survey.

"Tell us about your recent experience!"

It's STILL happening. I'm literally three feet from the door. Calm down.

I haven't even processed the receipt yet. I need space. It's not you - it's you.

Companies chase feedback like it's oxygen. Every tiny purchase becomes a corporate therapy session.

## The Survey That Is Never Five Minutes

Every survey claims:

"This will only take 3-5 minutes!"

Lies.

Suddenly you're trapped answering 22 questions about things you absolutely did not notice:

"How satisfied were you with the lighting in the knife aisle?"
"How would you rate the emotional support provided by our cashier?"
"How did our store layout impact your journey today?"

Journey?
I bought cat litter. I wasn't trekking the Oregon Trail.
The only trail I was on was "Get in, get out, avoid humanity."

Skip too many questions and the survey guilt-trips you:

"Are you sure you don't want to tell us MORE?"

Yes.
I am sure.

Leave me alone.

## The Star Rating Hostage Situation

Every gig-economy worker warns you:

"If it's anything less than five stars, please let me know!"

Translation:
"A four-star review will destroy my livelihood."

We're not rating service.
We're negotiating someone's survival inside a broken system.

It's psychological hostage-taking disguised as customer engagement.

I shouldn't need negotiation training to buy a burrito.

# Surveys Don't Improve Anything

Companies swear:

"Your feedback helps us improve!"

Improve what?
Your ability to track my shopping patterns?

Surveys exist to:
mine your data,
generate fake metrics,
fill corporate dashboards,
give middle managers something to present in meetings no one listens to.

None of this improves my sock-buying experience. Not one bit.

No executive has ever said:

"Harry said the bathroom was dirty - let's rebuild our entire business model!"

That is not a thing.

# Things That Should NEVER Ask for Feedback

We have gone off the cliff.

Today, you are asked to review:
self-checkout machines,
gas pumps,
chatbots,

restrooms,
microwaves at the gas station,
your pharmacy hemorrhoid cream acquisition,
the very concept of walking into a store.

We're one update away from toilets asking:

"Please rate your flushing experience!"

I'm begging you. No.

## The Absolute Worst Survey Attack I've Endured

I once bought a single bottle of water from a convenience store.
That's it. A universal human necessity. Transaction time: 14 seconds.

By the time I reached my car:

Buzz.
"How was your checkout experience?"

I ignore it.

Buzz.
"We noticed you didn't complete our survey!"

YOU NOTICED?
It's been 45 seconds.

Buzz.
"Your feedback helps us improve!"

Improve WHAT?
Your water-handing technique?

I get home.
Three more emails.

Then the next morning - A TEXT.

"We're sorry we didn't meet your expectations yesterday."

Expectations?
My expectation was "water is wet."

Mission accomplished.

At that point I half expected the manager to call me personally:

"We just want to grow from this experience. Where did WE go wrong?"

This right here?

This is why we can't have nice things.

## Why Survey Culture Pisses Me Off

Because I don't owe corporations emotional labor.

I'm not:
your therapist,
your consultant,
your motivational coach,
your relationship partner,
or the answer key to your quarterly KPIs.

If your business model depends on me filling out weekly report cards, maybe the issue isn't my lack of feedback.

Maybe the issue…
is your business.

## Why This Chapter Matters

Survey culture isn't annoying because companies want feedback.
It's annoying because companies want *you* to do the emotional labor they should be doing themselves.

This chapter matters because it highlights a truth we've all silently accepted:

Businesses are outsourcing accountability to the customer.

Instead of:
improving service,
training employees,
reducing wait times,
fixing broken systems,
or offering fair prices…

…they shove the responsibility back onto you through:
endless emails,
receipt novels,
push notifications,
and surveys disguised as "conversations."

Your role stops being "customer"
and becomes "unpaid consultant."

Surveys aren't about improvement.
They're about data mining, metric padding, and pretending a spreadsheet represents human experience.

And the constant demand for feedback doesn't create better businesses -
it creates burnout.

People start ignoring surveys.
Companies panic and send more surveys.
The cycle gets worse.
Nothing improves.

Meanwhile, the people surveys supposedly "help" -
employees under impossible rating systems -
end up punished for anything less than perfection.

We're not being asked for opinions.
We're being dragged into a broken performance model nobody benefits from.

This chapter matters because it calls out the absurdity of a world where buying socks,
requires a post-event emotional debrief.

And every time a company begs you for validation, every time another push notification whines for your "experience rating," every time a receipt tries to recruit you into a survey cult, we're reminded again:

This is why we can't have nice things.

# CHAPTER 26 - The Death of Privacy and Why Everyone Seems Fine With It

There was a time - not even that long ago - when privacy was a basic expectation. You could live your life without your refrigerator reporting your eating schedule or your TV snitching on your late-night binge habits.

Privacy didn't fade away gently.
It was murdered.
Dragged into an alley, stabbed repeatedly by tech companies, and left in a ditch.

And the worst part?
Everybody else just shrugged.

This is why we can't have nice things.

## Your Phone Is Listening - Just Accept It

We all know our phones listen to us.
Not symbolically.
Not figuratively.
Literally.

You make one innocent comment like:
"Man, I could go for tacos."

And suddenly your phone jumps in like a clingy personal assistant:

"Taco restaurants near you!"

Great.
Now I'm hungry and uncomfortable.

People try to explain it away:
"Oh, it's not listening - it's just targeted advertising!"

Right.
And I'm the King of England.

It's completely normal for your phone to psychically detect that you're thinking about replacing your underwear?
Please.

If your phone were any more attentive, it would start recommending therapists.

## Apps Track You Like You're on Probation

Every app wants access to everything:
location,
contacts,
photos,
microphone,
camera,
whatever trauma you haven't worked through yet.

We've normalized surveillance like it's a loyalty program.

You download a flashlight app - a FLASHLIGHT - and it demands GPS access "for functionality."

Functionality?
It's pretending to be a lightbulb, not coordinating drone strikes.

And people still tap "Allow" because the app promises a 20% off coupon.

Privacy: sold to the lowest bidder.

# The Sticker That Cost Me My Privacy

I recently bought a sticker.
A single sticker.
The kind of purchase that, historically, required zero documentation unless you were collecting receipts for the IRS as a particularly unhinged scrapbooker.
But the cashier asked the now-standard, soul-draining question: "Would you like your receipt texted or emailed?"

Not "Do you *want* a receipt?"
Oh no. That ship sailed years ago.
We've moved straight to *choosing the method by which we will be digitally haunted.*

And without thinking - like a trained lab rat who hears a bell and salivates - I typed my email.
For a sticker.

A sticker.

I didn't even want the receipt. What was I going to do with it? File it under "Important Financial Documents I Will Definitely Never Look At Again"?
But now, because I momentarily forgot how society works, I received three emails in less than an hour.
Three.
From a store whose entire business model revolves around selling quirky stationery and overpriced water bottles.

The first email was my receipt.
The second was a coupon I will never use.
The third was a desperate, emotionally unstable follow-up asking me to "rate my shopping experience," as if my epic sticker-buying journey belongs in the Library of Congress.

This is how they get you.
Not with major purchases.
Not with contracts.
Not with solemn, meaningful transactions.
But with a $2.99 impulse buy that now guarantees I will spend the next seven years clicking "unsubscribe," only for them to reply:
"We're sorry to see you go! Are you sure you want fewer emails?"
Yes.
I am unbelievably sure.
And this, ladies and gentlemen…

This is why we can't have nice things.

## Smart TVs: The Narc in Your Living Room

Smart TVs are spies with screens.

They listen.
They track.
They log every show you watch and every questionable choice you make at 1 a.m.

All so advertisers can whisper:
"He watches true crime alone in the dark… market him depression snacks."

Some of them even have cameras.

Why?
Why does my TV need to look at me?

Show me things - don't study me.
I don't need my Samsung analyzing my posture or filming me eat cereal out of the box at midnight.

That's not data.
That's blackmail material.
Mind your business, television.

## People Surrender Privacy Like It's a Hobby

Corporate surveillance is horrifying, but the public?
They've basically started offering privacy on a buy-one-get-one.

People film everything:
their home,
their kids,
their arguments,
their badge at work,
their license plate,
their EXACT LOCATION in real time.

Then they get confused when creeps show up in their inbox:
"How did you find me?!"

Linda,
You did a full Zillow tour of your house on Instagram.
You geotagged your living room.
Your entire personality is a live broadcast.

Some people are basically speedrunning towards getting kidnapped.

# The Moment I Realized Privacy Was Fully Dead

I once casually mentioned - out loud - that I needed a new pillow.
No typing.
No Googling.
No searching.

Just words floating through the air.
Two hours later, I open Instagram:
"STRUGGLING WITH NECK PAIN? TRY OUR ERGONOMIC MEMORY FOAM PILLOW!"

Excuse me?

At first, I thought maybe it was coincidence.
Maybe capitalism had guessed correctly.

But then - and I swear this happened - the next ad said:
"People over 35 need better sleep support."

My phone age-shamed me.
Then Facebook joined in:
"New pillow? Here are 15 affordable options!"

Then Amazon chimed in:
"Still thinking about pillows?"

NO, AMAZON, I WAS TRYING NOT TO.

It felt like I was being stalked by a Bed Bath & Beyond employee with mystical powers.

And the ads kept getting more personal:
"Pillowcases that match your pillow-shopping personality!"

"You look tired. Try this one."

YOU LOOK TIRED??
My phone is negging me now?

That's when I knew:
Privacy isn't dying.
It's dead, decomposed, and currently being sold to third-party advertisers for twelve cents a data point.

This is why we can't have nice things.

## Companies Sell Your Data Like It's a Side Hustle

Your data gets traded like middle-school baseball cards.
Search one thing?
Click one thing?
Merely think about one thing?
Congratulations - seven companies now know your snack preferences and emotional stability.

Every business swears:
"We take your privacy seriously."

Absolutely.
Right up until someone offers them forty bucks and a coupon code.

## A Modern Field Guide to Surveillance Creatures

Here are the main offenders you encounter daily:

**The Always-Listening Smartphone**
Eavesdrops like a nosy aunt.

**The Data-Harvesting Ap**
Why does Sudoku need microphone access?

**The Smart TV That Knows Too Much**
Knows your habits better than your spouse.

**The Voice Assistant That Pretends Not to Judge You**
Alexa absolutely heard you crying into leftover pizza rolls.

**The Loyalty Card That Sells Your Soul**
Buy one vape and suddenly 14 companies know your birthdate.

**Your Car**
Tracks everything except your happiness.

**Your Neighbor's Doorbell Camera**
Congrats - you're an unpaid background actor in every delivery video they post.

# "If You're Not Doing Anything Wrong…" - The Dumbest Take Ever Invented

Ah yes.
The privacy philosophers.

"If you're not doing anything wrong, why care?"

That sentence has the intellectual weight of eating soup with a fork.

Privacy isn't about hiding wrongdoing.
It's about dignity.

It's about not being monitored because you binge-watched trash TV at 2 a.m.

Saying "I don't need privacy because I'm not doing anything wrong" is like saying:

"I don't need curtains - I'm not getting dressed illegally."

Please sit down.

## We Traded Privacy for Convenience - And Lost Badly

The truth is, we weren't robbed.
We traded privacy away.

We exchanged it for:
faster shipping,
digital coupons,
voice assistants,
smart bulbs,
food delivery recommendations.

We bartered autonomy for the privilege of yelling "Order paper towels!" at a glowing cylinder that misunderstands us 40% of the time.

We didn't even get a good deal.

## The Horror Is Funny Because the Battle Is Already Lost

Here's the unnerving part:
Nothing shocks people anymore.

Fifteen years ago, if you said:
"Your fridge will monitor your eating habits,"
people would've called the police.

Today?

"Oooh, does it sync with my smartwatch?"

Privacy isn't just dead.
It's cremated and stored in the cloud.

And we just keep scrolling.

Because honestly?

This is why we can't have nice things.

## Why This Chapter Matters

Privacy didn't quietly slip away.
It was taken - aggressively, systematically, enthusiastically.

And worse?
We participated.

Every time we approve a request for access,
every time a device listens without permission,
every time an app demands information it doesn't need,
every time we broadcast our entire lives to strangers,

we normalize a world where being monitored is the price of existing.

This chapter isn't just a rant.
It's a wake-up call.

Because if privacy becomes optional,
what happens to:
individuality?
safety?
dignity?
the right to exist without being analyzed?

Every time your phone predicts your thoughts,
every time your TV studies your habits,
every time someone livestreams their Tuesday night meltdown,
every time your data gets sold before you finish a sentence -

we drift further into a world where nothing is personal
and everything is content.

And as always:

This is why we can't have nice things.

**PART III - THINGS THAT SHOULDN'T PISS ME OFF...
BUT TOTALLY DO**
Minor annoyances that feel like personal attacks.

# CHAPTER 27 - People Who Can't Park

There are a lot of things wrong with modern civilization, but if you really want to see the soul of a society, don't look at its laws, leaders, or infrastructure.

Look at the parking lot.

Parking lots are X-rays for human character. No filters. No pretense. No inspirational quotes. Just raw evidence that a shocking number of adults cannot do the one thing the DMV begged them to master: put a vehicle between two painted lines.

It's not complicated.
It's not abstract.
It's not calculus or neurosurgery.

It is:

Here is a rectangle.
Please place your vehicle inside it.

And yet, every single day, you pull into a lot and see proof that we, as a species, are not ready for any more technological advancement.

Self-driving cars?
Half these people haven't mastered self-parking yet.

We're out here dreaming about autonomous fleets and robotic chauffer's while Ray from Lot B can't even center his Corolla without turning it into modern art.

Maybe - and hear me out - we should master Level 1 parking before we attempt Level 5 autonomy.

This is why we can't have nice things.

## The Crooked Parkers

Let's start with the most common offender: the diagonally challenged.

The lot is full of neat rows, clean lines, uniform spacing. Then here comes this hero, sliding in at a 27-degree angle like they're docking a space shuttle in a storm.

Half in one space, half in the next.

Back tire in one zip code, front bumper in another.

They get out of the car, glance at their handiwork... and just walk away. No guilt. No shame. No attempt to fix it. They look at the chaos they've created and think:

"Yeah. Nailed it."

And now, because of them, three other people can't park. Some poor soul in a normal-sized car gives up and leaves because the angle of this jackass's Camry has created a geometry problem NASA wouldn't attempt.

We've all had a slightly crooked park now and then. You misjudge, the line is faded, the sun's in your eyes, whatever. The difference is a functional adult sees that, sighs, and fixes it.

The chronic crooked parker does not believe in correction. They believe in vibes.

# The Oversized Truck Bully

Then there's the oversized truck guy.

Important caveat:
Not everyone with a big truck is a parking menace. Some are decent humans who park like they're aware other life forms exist.

But you know exactly the type I'm talking about.

The dude with the lifted, extended-cab, walk-up-three-steps-to-enter behemoth of a truck that looks like it was designed to drag boulders up a mountain, but somehow spends 95% of its time at Target.

He has:
tires taller than your torso,
a light bar bright enough to communicate with the International Space Station,
and a "NO FEAR" sticker that tells you everything you need to know about his sense of responsibility.

He does not see parking spaces as guidelines.
He sees them as suggestions.

The truck is huge, but the self-awareness driving it is fun-sized.
This man bought a vehicle big enough to transport livestock but parks it with the confidence of someone who just learned what mirrors are.

One of two things usually happens:
He takes two spots on purpose, dead center over the line, because his truck is apparently too "special" to risk mingling with civilian vehicles.
He crams that monster into a single spot but leaves zero room on either side, so anyone unlucky enough to be next to him gets to practice contortionist-level door exits.

And if you happen to be parked next to him when you come back?

You just stand there looking at your own car like, "Cool. Guess I live here now. This is my home."

And of course, this kind of parking terrorism always spreads - one badly-parked truck inspires three more people to give up and follow suit. A full parking-lot domino effect.

This is why we can't have nice things.

## The Human Door Ding

Then we have the people who technically park between the lines, but only because it brings them closer to their true calling: door dinging the hell out of your car.

Their parking job is fine.

Centered.
Straight.
Respectable.

But then they fling their door open like it's a battering ram and your car is a medieval castle gate.

No hesitation.

No awareness.

No understanding that other people's vehicles are not, in fact, padded.

You come back to your car, see a new little chip in your paint, and just know: someone treated your door like bumpers at a bowling alley.

# The "I Make My Own Space" People

Parking lots have lines for a reason.

Some people see those lines and think, "Rules."
Others see them and think, "Art direction."

These are the people who:
park at the end of a row but slightly into the driving lane,
park on the hash marks between handicapped spaces like they discovered a secret bonus spot,
park in front of clearly marked NO PARKING - FIRE LANE zones as if the word "NO" was purely decorative.

They are the spiritual cousins of people who stand directly in doorways or stop at the bottom of escalators.

Someone could literally be trying to drive through a clearly marked lane and these geniuses will leave their car there with hazard lights on like that suddenly makes it legal.

Hazard lights are not a "pause life" button.

They do not create invisible permission.

You're not in an emergency.

You're in Starbucks.

# Parallel Parking: The Ultimate Skill Check

Parallel parking is the boss battle of driving.

It's not impossible.

It just requires awareness, patience, and a basic understanding of angles.

So naturally, we as a society have collectively decided: absolutely not.

People pull up to a parallel spot with 1.5 times the length of their car and still bail out like, "Nah, there's no way." Or worse, they try once, panic halfway in, and then leave their vehicle at a weird half-committed angle - rear end hanging into traffic, front wheel kissing the curb like it owes it money.

If parallel parking were televised, it would be categorized as horror.

Every car commercial shows someone gliding into a tight space with ballet-level precision.

Meanwhile, the rest of us are out here doing 27-point turns like we're docking a submarine in a kiddie pool.

## Revenge Fantasies and Sarcastic Notes

If you've ever pulled into a lot, seen some absolutely heinous parking crime, and felt a powerful urge to leave a note, you are not alone.

We all have that moment where we imagine ourselves as the hero of the parking lot - the one who fights injustice with a ballpoint pen and a sticky note.

Most of the time, you mutter under your breath and go about your day like a functioning adult.

But the fantasy?

It lives rent free.

You imagine writing:
"You park like the lines personally insulted your family."
"Just curious: is your car allergic to being straight?"
"I see the 'P' on your gearshift doesn't stand for 'Practice.'"
"Just checking - did the lines hurt your feelings, or is this a conceptual art piece?"
"If confidence were accuracy, you'd be a god."

Every once in a while, the fantasy wins.

You've had a long day. You're tired. Your patience is fumes. You see a truck taking up three spots, diagonally, in front of a store packed with people circling like vultures.

That's when you grab a scrap of paper from your glovebox and leave something like:

"Congratulations on being the main character in this parking lot."

Do they read it?
Do they care?
Do they even notice?

Probably not.

But sometimes, the note isn't for them.

It's for you.
Proof that you haven't completely surrendered to the chaos.

---

# The Types of Bad Parkers

For clarity, a quick taxonomy:

**The Diagonal Disaster**
Cannot enter a space in a straight line. Always at an angle like the earth is tilting beneath their car.

**The Line Straddler**
Dead center on the line. Not in one spot, not in the other. Schrödinger's parker.

**The Space Hoarder**
Takes two spots on purpose to "protect their car," as if that justifies being an inconsiderate menace.

**The Curb Climber**
Half in the spot, half experiencing off-road terrain on the curb. Somehow proud of this.

**The Door Slapper**
Perfectly parked, morally bankrupt. Uses your car as a stopping mechanism for their door.

**The Fire Lane Philosopher**
Believes rules do not apply if they'll "only be a minute." Their entire moral framework is built on that sentence.

**The Invisible Trailer**
Leaves three car lengths of space in front "just in case" they need to swing out like they're hauling a forty-foot trailer. They are not.

**The Emotional Support Truck**
Big vehicle, tiny self-awareness. Takes up maximum space both physically and spiritually.

You can spot at least three of these every time you go anywhere with more than eight parking spots.

# The Real Reason Bad Parking Is So Infuriating

On the surface, it seems petty.

Who cares if someone is slightly over the line? Who cares if they take up a little extra space?

You care.
I care.
Most people with functioning brains care.

Because parking isn't just about spots.
It's about consideration.

It's one of the simplest ways we interact with strangers. We'll never meet them, never know their names, never speak to them - but we share space with them. We navigate around each other. We either inconvenience or accommodate each other.

Good parking says:

"I know other people exist."

Bad parking says:

"It's just me out here. Everyone else is background."

And that's what pisses us off.

Every crooked car, every line-straddler, every truck stretched across two and a half spaces is a reminder that some people are moving through the world like they're the only ones in it.

# Why People Who Can't Park Piss Me Off (More Than They Should)

It's not just the inconvenience.
It's not just trying to wedge your car into the half-spot leftover by someone else's incompetence.

It's what it represents.

People who can't park - and won't fix it - are part of the same club as:
the people who block aisles with their carts and don't move,
the people who blast speakerphone calls in public,
the people who ignore "DO NOT ENTER" signs because they're in a hurry.

It's all the same attitude:

"My time matters. My convenience matters. Yours? Eh."

So yeah, it's "just parking."

But it's also everything.

It's the visible symptom of a deeper disease: a massive number of people who are physically grown, legally licensed, and emotionally three steps from licking windows.

And every time I watch someone abandon their crooked car and stroll away like they didn't just create a cascading inconvenience for six other people, that familiar wave of irritation hits:

This is why we can't have nice things.

# Why This Chapter Matters

Bad parking feels stupid to get mad about.

It feels petty.
Small.
Unimportant.

And that's exactly why it works as a perfect stress test.

Parking lots are one of the last places where strangers are expected to cooperate without supervision. No authority figures. No enforcement most of the time. Just an unspoken agreement that we'll all do the bare minimum so everyone can get on with their day.

No speeches.
No meetings.
No apps.
No rules beyond two painted lines.

When someone ignores even that, it hits harder than it should - not because the inconvenience is catastrophic, but because it confirms a suspicion most of us already carry:

That the social contract is thinning.
That consideration is optional.
That too many people move through shared spaces assuming friction is everyone else's problem.

This chapter isn't about geometry.

It's about the emotional whiplash of realizing how little effort cooperation actually requires - and how often it's still refused.

That's why bad parking lingers.

Not because of the spot.

But because it's one more quiet reminder that modern life asks less and less of people…

… and somehow still gets disappointed.

And when irritation stacks up over enough small moments like that?

Yeah.
You end up pissed off.

This is why we can't have nice things.

# CHAPTER 28 - Adults Who Microwave Fish in Public

There are many types of people in this world, but none reveal their true moral character faster than the ones who willingly, knowingly, and with premeditated malice microwave fish in a shared space.

Microwaving fish at work is not a mistake.
It's not an accident.
It's not a cultural misunderstanding.

It is olfactory terrorism.

There is no fish that smells good once microwaved. None. Even fish that tasted amazing the night before become biological weapons the moment they spin in a breakroom microwave.

The smell doesn't drift - it invades.
It creeps out of the microwave like cursed fog from a horror movie, slides under cubicles, coats the air vents, and seeps into the fabric of every office chair.

It's not an odor.
It's a presence.
The kind of presence that needs to be saged out of the building.

And the person who did it?
They walk away from the microwave like nothing happened.

No remorse.
No shame.
No second thoughts.

This is why we can't have nice things.

## The Olfactory Attack Heard 'Round the Office

There is nothing more demoralizing than walking into the workplace kitchen at noon, hungry and hopeful, thinking about that sandwich you packed... only to have your nostrils assaulted by reheated salmon that died during the Carter administration.

The smell hits you like a physical force.

You stagger back.
Your eyes water.
Your appetite collapses into itself like a dying star.

And in the middle of this gastronomic apocalypse stands the culprit - calmly eating their steaming plate of fish like they didn't just gas an entire department.

You look at them, waiting for any sign of guilt.
Nothing.

They're chewing that salmon like they're on a romantic date overlooking the ocean.

Meanwhile, the rest of the office is quietly evacuating.

## The Day the Office Died

One workplace I was in had a guy named Ron. Everyone has a Ron.

Ron wasn't a bad guy. Friendly. Held doors open. Brought donuts on Fridays.

But Ron had one fatal flaw:
Ron loved leftover tilapia.

One day, Ron microwaved tilapia in the breakroom at 11:57 a.m.

That's prime lunchtime.
That's rush hour.
That's fish-bomb o'clock.

The smell exploded out of the microwave like it had been waiting to escape.

By 12:03, people were gagging in the hallway.
By 12:06, the entire building smelled like an aquarium declared bankruptcy.
By 12:10, HR sent an all-staff email titled: "Friendly Reminder About Strong-Smelling Foods."

Ron never admitted guilt.

He just sat there silently eating his fish while an entire office of adults collectively lost the will to live.

To this day, I swear the smell lingered for three business days and may have gained voting rights.

And honestly, this right here?

This is why we can't have nice things.

# Workplace Kitchen Etiquette Failures

Fish microwavers are the final boss, but they're not the only monsters in the breakroom.

Every office has:

### The Burnt Popcorn Arsonist
Burns popcorn every single time. Leaves the building smelling like someone cremated a stuffed animal. Acts surprised.

### The Leftover Hoarder
Their Tupperware from 2019 is still in the office fridge. It has evolved. It has a culture. It may qualify for citizenship.

### The Open-Container Soup Slurper
Brings soup in a container that leaks 100% of the time. The microwave looks like a crime scene.

### The Double-Portion Microwave Hog
Microwaves a 3-pound meal for 17 minutes while the rest of the office forms a queue like refugees waiting for aid.

### The "Someone Else Will Clean It" Specialist
Sauce everywhere. Splatter on the ceiling. Rice grains in the keypad. Walks away like the kitchen is a self-healing organism.

These are the people who genuinely believe kitchens clean themselves, like some kind of sentient Disney mop appears at night and handles it.

# Foods That Should Be Illegal in Breakrooms

Let's just make it official. Some foods should never be microwaved at work under any circumstances:

**Fish (all forms)**
If it swims, it stays home.

**Eggs**
Scrambled, hard-boiled, egg casserole - all turn into atmospheric war crimes.

**Broccoli**
Healthy, yes. Reheated in a shared microwave? Smells like the devil's compost pile.

**Curry**
Delicious at home. At work, it coats the air like a permanent spice fog.

**Anything With Garlic**
There should be a garlic quarantine rule. 24 hours minimum.

**Leftover Fast Food**
Reheated burgers smell like wet socks and regret.

**Anything in Styrofoam**
The scent of melting Styrofoam plus mystery food = felonies.

**Cabbage**
You already know.

**Anything described as "leftover seafood surprise"**
There are no surprises. Only suffering.

Call the list restrictive, call it oppressive, whatever you want. You can't call it wrong.

# The Psychology of the Public Fish Microwaver

Let's examine these people, because they're a fascinating species.

Public fish microwavers possess at least one of the following:
a broken shame reflex,
a belief that personal comfort outweighs communal suffering,
nostril blindness,
an inner peace that can only come from never having been told "please stop,"
a sociopathic level of calm in the face of mass disgust.

They are the same people who:
listen to videos on speakerphone,
clip their nails at their desk,
stand too close in line,
and think reheating shrimp scampi is a constitutional right.

These are people who walk through life with the unshakeable confidence of someone who has never once heard the word "no."

# The Aftermath

Once fish has been microwaved in a workspace, the environment never fully recovers.

Coworkers lose trust in each other.
Conversations get shorter.
People start bringing lunch from home so they don't have to risk entering the kitchen.

Someone from accounting opens a window even though it's 37 degrees outside.
The janitor refuses to go in without gloves.
The air becomes thick with tension - and fish. Mostly fish.

And just when everyone thinks the air has finally cleared...

Someone reheats shrimp at 9 a.m. and resets humanity's progress back to zero.

## Why Adults Who Microwave Fish Piss Me Off

Because it's avoidable.
Because it's inconsiderate.
Because it ruins the day for everyone else.
Because it's selfish at a molecular level.
Because it smells like Poseidon's armpit.

And because, once again:

This is why we can't have nice things.

## Why This Chapter Matters

Microwaving fish in public isn't really about fish.

It's about consideration.
Or, more accurately, the complete absence of it.

A reheated salmon cloud is never just an unfortunate smell.
It's a message.
A small but powerful signal that says:

"My comfort matters more than your air quality, your appetite, and your will to live."

This chapter matters because it exposes something bigger than a bad lunch choice.
It reveals how many adults move through the world with zero awareness of how their actions impact the people trapped around them.

The person who microwaves fish at work is the same person who yells on speakerphone, leaves messes in shared spaces, blocks the aisle, and behaves as if basic social etiquette is optional homework they decided not to turn in.

It's not the fish that bothers everyone.
It's the mindset behind it.

Shared spaces only function when people quietly agree to not make life miserable for each other.
It's a simple social contract: use the kitchen, don't commit olfactory war crimes.

When someone ignores that, it's not an accident.
It's who they are.

And that's why it sticks with people long after the smell fades.
Because it isn't just lunch.
It's a preview of how that person operates in every part of their life.

Every time someone nukes day-old tilapia and walks away like they didn't just trigger a building-wide evacuation, we get another reminder of the theme holding this whole book together:

This is why we can't have nice things.

# CHAPTER 29 - Small Talk: I Hate It Here

Small talk is society's greatest scam.

It is the conversational equivalent of packing peanuts - everywhere, useless, messy, and somehow still considered "necessary" by people who don't know how to function without narrating every waking moment.

We created entire civilizations, discovered electricity, invented the internet… and yet two adults standing near each other still say things like:

"Sure is chilly today."

Wow. Riveting stuff, Eleanor. The temperature changed. Please alert NASA.

Next, tell me clouds exist.

Small talk is the duct tape of social interaction - cheap, flimsy, universally applied, and completely unable to hold together anything of substance.

This is why we can't have nice things.

## The Ritual of Forced Pleasantries

There is a specific choreography to small talk - a dance nobody enjoys but everyone performs because society apparently collapses if two humans stand silently in the same room.

You must:
smile like you're being filmed,
nod like a bobblehead with a head injury,
ask about things you do not care about,
pretend to listen to answers you'll forget instantly.

It's emotional miming.

You're not connecting - you're checking a box.
And the box is labeled:

"Prevent awkwardness."

But here's the thing: small talk is the awkwardness.
We're not avoiding it - we're prolonging it.

## "Got Any Weekend Plans?" - The Question From Hell

Every Friday.
Every office.
Every coworker clinging to conversational scripts like they're performing in a middle school play.

"Got any weekend plans?"

Stop interrogating my personal life like you're writing a BuzzFeed listicle.

I barely have weekday plans. My plan is to not plan.

Once, when I told someone I had "no plans," they replied:

"Aww, maybe next weekend will be better!"

Better?

Maybe my plans are to sit silently and not talk to anyone - you know... bliss.

# The Buffet of Pointless Questions

One day, I was stuck in the lobby with a coworker named Heather - the kind of person who treats every passing human like an opportunity to host her own talk show.

In the three minutes before our meeting, Heather asked:

"How's your morning?"
"Busy week?"
"Crazy weather, huh?"
"How was traffic?"
"Plans for lunch?"
"Any fun for the weekend?"
"Sleeping okay?"
"You like that coffee place?"
"Ever tried almond milk?"
"Do you bake?"
"Did you see what Dawn from accounting posted?"
"Did you know Dawn bakes?"
"Do you bake?" (again)

At one point, I'm pretty sure she asked how often I floss.

I blacked out around minute two.

This wasn't a conversation - it was cardio.

## The Awkward Conversation Archetypes

Small talk wouldn't be complete without the cast of characters who specialize in making it worse:

**The Weather Reporter**
Provides meteorological updates like God hired them personally.

**The Oversharer**
You say, "How are you?"
They answer, "My dog has diarrhea and my ex just blocked me again."

**The One-Upper**
You walked a mile?
They climbed Everest. Twice. Barefoot. In the snow.

**The Robot**
Asks the same three questions to everyone every day like an HR chatbot with legs.

**The Pauser**
Takes so long to answer that you start reviewing every decision you've ever made.

**The Close-Talker**
Gets so close you can feel their breath participating in the conversation.

**The Interrogator**
Turns small talk into a police interview.
"So where are you from? How long? Do you like it? What's your blood type?"

**The Nervous Laughter Person**
Laughs at nouns.
Laughs at adjectives.
Laughs at silence.

**The Repeat Questioner**
Ask's "How's your day?" twice because they weren't listening the first time.

**The Overly Detailed Weather Enthusiast**
Pulls out Doppler data like you asked them to brief NOAA.

**The Bathroom Talker**
Attempts conversation at the sink, the urinal, or the stall. Should be deported to another office immediately.

Every time someone tries to chat with me at a urinal, I'm reminded all over again:

This is why we can't have nice things.

## Small Talk at Work - A Unique Form of Hell

The workplace is where small talk thrives like mold.
The coffee machine? Forced small talk arena.
The printer? Bonding-through-misery station.
The breakroom? Small Talk Thunderdome.

The hallways are the worst. You try to walk. They stop walking. Now you're talking diagonally like two malfunctioning Roombas.

And nothing tops restroom conversation.

If you talk to me while I'm washing my hands, we are no longer coworkers - we are enemies.

## Small Talk Gone Horribly Wrong

Sometimes, small talk mutates into something unholy - a spontaneous heart-to-heart nobody asked for.

The worst cases include:
accidentally triggering someone's life story,
someone answering your polite question with generational trauma,
someone asking follow-up questions you are not emotionally prepared to answer,
someone laughing WAY too loud at something not even remotely funny,
someone dropping a casual horror line like:
"Yeah, my cat died and also I'm on a juice cleanse."

Small talk is like walking through a minefield: you never know which step will blow up in your face.

## Why Small Talk Pisses Me Off

Because it's theatrical nonsense.
Because it adds zero value to human existence.
Because it wastes time.
Because it turns adults into malfunctioning puppets.
Because it's the human equivalent of clicking "I agree" on terms and conditions you didn't read.

Every "How's your day going?" deserves the real answer:

"It was fine until this conversation started."

Pretending to be interested is exhausting.
Silence should not be treated like a crime scene.
We have finite time on this earth - and we're spending it discussing cloud coverage.

## Small Talk Questions That Should Be Illegal

**"How's work?"**
We are AT work. You know how work is. This is entrapment.

**"Got any weekend plans?"**
Stop asking me this like you're taking a census.

**"Busy today?"**
No, I just carry papers around for fun.

**"Hot enough for ya?"**
Nobody has ever enjoyed answering this.

**"Cold enough for ya?"**
Winter edition of the same crime.

**"How's your morning going?"**
It's 8:03 a.m. Nothing is going.

**"You look tired - everything okay?"**
Arrest this person immediately.

**"What's new?"**
Nothing. There is never anything new. Ever.

**"Big plans tonight?"**
If it's after 4 p.m., the answer is always no.

**"Long day?"**
Brother, it's America. Every day is a long day.

**"How are things?"**
Things are things. Let's move on.

**"Can you believe this weather?"**
Yes. Because it happens daily.

**"How's the family?"**
Too complicated for hallway conversation.

**"How was your weekend?"**
You want the lie, not the truth.

**Any question asked in the bathroom.**
Punishable by exile.

## Why This Chapter Matters

Small talk isn't meaningless because the topics are small.
It's meaningless because the connection is.

We pretend it's polite conversation,
but really it's the social version of busywork -
words for the sake of words.

This chapter matters because it exposes the truth we all feel but rarely say out loud:
small talk exhausts people.
It drains energy instead of building it.
It replaces authenticity with a script everyone hates performing.

Small talk isn't about weather or weekends.
It's about avoiding silence.
It's about avoiding depth.
It's about avoiding each other while pretending we're not.

It shows how uncomfortable people are with real conversation -
how quickly we retreat into clichés -
instead of curiosity.

It creates interactions that feel forced, hollow, and pointless,
leaving everyone involved a little more tired,
a little more irritated,
and a little more convinced that humans were a bad idea.

And that matters, because when fake conversations fill our days,
there's no room left for the real ones.

Small talk isn't harmless.
It's noise.
It's filler.
It's the illusion of connection masquerading as the real thing.

And every time someone corners you with,
"So, uh… got any plans for the weekend?,"
while both of you silently pray for a sinkhole,
you're reminded once again:

This is why we can't have nice things.

# CHAPTER 30 - Unsolicited Advice and Other Forms of Torture

There are many forms of human suffering: heartbreak, taxes, airport security, stepping on Legos, watching someone microwave fish at work - but none compare to the spiritual violation known as unsolicited advice.

Nothing makes my eye twitch faster than hearing the five most dangerous words in the English language:

"You know what you should…"

No.

No, I don't.

And more importantly - I didn't ask.

Unsolicited advice is the perfect storm of arrogance, delusion, and the overwhelming belief that someone else's life would run better if the advisor were appointed temporary dictator.

This is why we can't have nice things.

# The Unsolicited Advice People (UAPs)

UAPs roam the earth believing they were put here to guide the rest of us peasants toward enlightenment we never requested. They give advice the way raccoons dig through trash - aggressively and without boundaries.

Three universal truths about unsolicited advice:
It is never helpful.
It is always condescending.
It is always delivered by someone you would never hire as a consultant.

UAPs approach you with the confidence of a surgeon and the accuracy of a drunk archer.

# The Great Fitness Intervention of 2017

I once had a coworker - let's call him Brad, because of course his name was Brad - who was deep into CrossFit.

Brad's personality consisted of:
CrossFit,
talking about CrossFit,
recruiting victims into CrossFit.

One day, I made the grave mistake of existing near him while holding a protein bar.

A normal human would say, "Hey, that looks good," and move on.

Not Brad.

Brad saw the protein bar and declared:

"Hey man, you know what you should do? Switch to intermittent fasting while incorporating three HIIT cycles a day. It'll transform your whole life."

Brad, my man, I am just trying to survive Tuesday. I do not need your unsolicited personal training, dietary restructuring, or spiritual awakening.

He then launched into his entire regimen - in detail - for a full eleven minutes.

I aged.
My soul left my body, got coffee, came back, and he was still talking.

That was the moment I realized: unsolicited advice isn't a flaw. It's a lifestyle.

## The Grocery Store Incident

Another time, I was standing in a grocery line - minding my business, buying normal human items like bread and deodorant - when the stranger behind me leaned in and said:

"You know what you should do? Switch to a plant-based diet. It changed my life."

Sir, I don't know you.
I don't want to know you.
And if I wanted nutritional wisdom from a man wearing Crocs with socks, I'd have gone looking.

He started unloading his entire dietary journey:
"Cutting dairy will transform your skin."
"Almond milk is basically a superfood."
"If you combine spinach, chia, and bee pollen… "

My guy, your cart is full of frozen taquitos. You are in no position to advise anyone.

Then - and I swear this happened - he picked up the loaf of bread I was holding.

Picked. It. Up.

Looked me dead in the eye and said:

"Bread is just filler. Your gut biome will thank you if you cut this out."

First of all, put my bread back.
Second, my gut biome and I have an understanding.
Third, the only person allowed to touch my groceries is the cashier, and even they look underpaid to do it.

He ended with:

"You'll thank me later."

No. I will not.
I will think about this moment on my deathbed and still be annoyed.

This is why we can't have nice things.

## The Worst Offenders: Fitness Evangelists

Fitness evangelists are the Jehovah's Witnesses of wellness. They materialize out of nowhere to critique your lunch.

Eating a sandwich?

"Carbs are poison."

Drinking water?

"That brand isn't alkaline."

Doing literally nothing?

"You know, sitting is the new smoking."

Fitness evangelists assume you're one inspirational quote away from joining their cult.

They speak in absolutes:
"You must do keto."
"You must lift."
"You must cold plunge."
"You must train like a Spartan warrior recovering from emotional trauma."

Meanwhile, half of them look like they've been one squat away from a spinal injury since 2016.

## Parenting Advice From Non-Parents (The Ultimate Crime)

There is no more dangerous, delusional creature than a childless adult giving parenting advice.

Parents barely know what they're doing - and they're in the arena, fighting tiny chaos goblins.

Non-parents confidently say things like:

"Kids need structure. You just have to be firm."

Firm?

Ma'am, I saw a toddler punch a grocery cart and win.

Or:

"I would never let my kid throw a tantrum in public."

Your imaginary kid behaves beautifully.
Your imaginary kid doesn't eat crayons.
Your imaginary kid says, "Thank you for the boundaries!"

Real kids?

Real kids eat gravel and scream at pigeons.

Non-parents giving parenting advice are like people who watched one YouTube video about flying a plane and now think they're ready to land a 747.

# The "You Should Invest This Way" Guy

Knows nothing about money, still gives advice like he manages Warren Buffett's checking account.

He recommends:
silver,
gold bars,
crypto,
crypto backed by silver,
vending machine empires,
"passive income strategies" that are mostly pyramid schemes.

He ends every sentence with:

"Trust me."

I do not trust you.

## "Quit Your Job and Follow Your Passion!" People

These advisors always suggest you take massive risks they would never dream of taking.

"Quit your job! Start a bakery! Open an Etsy shop! Become a life coach!"

You first, Lucille.

## The DIY Advisor

Believes everything can be cured with essential oils and vinegar.

Got anxiety?

"Lavender."

Car won't start?

"Try peppermint."

Marriage trouble?

"Tea tree oil."

Sir, I need therapy, not a salad dressing.

## The Opinion Sniper

Sits silently until you mention literally anything, then swoops in:

"Oh, you're going to Hawaii? You know what you should do…"

Disappear.
That's what you should do.

## Why Unsolicited Advice Pisses Me Off

Because it's intrusive.
Because it's condescending.
Because it assumes you're an idiot in need of guidance.
Because it turns every interaction into an unsolicited TED Talk.
Because the people giving the most advice are the least qualified to give it.

And because - say it with me:

This is why we can't have nice things.

## Why This Chapter Matters

Unsolicited advice isn't about helping people.
It's about control.
It's about ego.
It's about someone deciding their opinion needs to live inside your life without being invited.

Every time someone gives advice you didn't ask for, they're sending a message:
*"I know better than you."*

And that's what gets under your skin - not the suggestion, but the assumption behind it.

It's never the experts doing it.
It's never the people you'd actually trust.
It's always the Brads of the world, handing out life strategies like expired coupons.

Unsolicited advice turns normal interactions into evaluations.
It treats your choices like mistakes.
It treats your boundaries like optional.
It treats your life like a group project you didn't sign up for.

And the worst part?
The people who give the most advice are the ones least qualified to run their own lives, let alone yours.

This chapter matters because everyone knows what it feels like to be cornered by someone who's "just trying to help" while making everything worse. It's exhausting. It's intrusive. And it's one more reminder that some people don't understand the concept of staying in their lane.

Which is exactly why:

This is why we can't have nice things.

# CHAPTER 31 - Why I Don't Trust Anyone Who Says "Circle Back"

There are red flags in life you can't ignore.
If someone says, "No offense, but…" you're about to be offended.
If someone says, "I'm a straight shooter," they're about to lie to you in a spiral.

But the biggest red flag of them all?

"Let's circle back."

No phrase triggers my fight-or-flight faster. "Circle back" isn't communication - it's a corporate smoke bomb. A linguistic fire drill designed to sound responsible while guaranteeing absolutely nothing happens.

Because in corporate language, "let's circle back" doesn't mean "later."
It means:
I'm avoiding this.
I hope you forget.
Future You can deal with this hot mess.
If we never speak of it again, that'd be great.

It's corporate ghosting, but with email invites.

And every time I hear someone say it with a straight face, I'm reminded all over again:

This is exactly why we can't have nice things.

## The Meeting Where Productivity Went to Die

I once attended a meeting where someone said "circle back" nine times.
NINE.
I counted. I wrote it down like a court stenographer documenting crimes.

The meeting was supposed to solve a single technical issue. One question. One problem. One fix. But the moment the first "circle back" dropped, the discussion flatlined.

By "circle back" number three, the idea had been murdered.
By number nine, we were holding a quiet memorial service for accountability.

At the end, someone cheerfully said:

"Great progress today, team."

Progress?
We didn't identify a problem.
We didn't assign an owner.
We didn't decide a damn thing.

The only thing we circled was the drain - and even that took three subcommittees and a follow-up meeting to confirm,

This is why I don't trust anyone who says "circle back."
Because it means: Not. A. Damn. Thing.

# Corporate Jargon: The Language of Cowards

Plain English is dangerous in the office. It's too clear. Too direct. Too traceable.
So instead, people hide behind Buzzword Teflon - a protective layer of nonsense that keeps responsibility from sticking to them.

The toolkit includes:
"Let's take this offline." Translation: I want fewer witnesses.
"Let's touch base." Translation: I crave the illusion of productivity.
"We'll revisit that." Translation: No, we won't.
"We're aligned." Translation: We are profoundly not aligned.
"I hear you." Translation: I am actively ignoring you.

Corporate jargon isn't communication - it's hiding in plain sight while pretending to be useful.

Corporate jargon is basically hostage negotiation, but with more dry-erase markers.

This is why we can't have nice things.

# If "Circle Back" Were a Person

Imagine "Circle Back" as an employee:
Arrives 10 minutes late every day,
Carries a notebook but writes nothing,
Nods aggressively during meetings,
Volunteers to "own the follow-up" but disappears,
Takes 90-minute lunches "for morale,"
Has a meeting whenever you need answers,
Gets promoted annually for reasons unknown to medical science,
If he had a spirit animal, it would be an empty calendar invite with no agenda and no purpose.

If "circle back" were human, HR would warn you:

"Please stop assigning him tasks. He's not built for that."

## Middle Managers: Buzzword Pokémon Trainers

Middle managers collect buzzwords like rare cards.
They don't communicate - they deploy terminology.

Their holy grail sentence is:

"Let's circle back and touch base to ensure we have the bandwidth to leverage synergies."

Zero ideas.
Zero action.
One smoothie of empty syllables.

## Buzzwords That Should Be Illegal

**"Circle back."**
Translation: If you remember this later, that's on you.

**"Low-hanging fruit."**
Translation: We're lazy.

**"Bandwidth."**
Translation: I'm overwhelmed and want to sound technical.

**"Synergy."**
Translation: Two bad ideas pretending to be one good one.

**"Hop on a quick call."**
Translation: Prepare to waste 20 minutes.

**"Right-size the workforce."**
Translation: We're firing people but want it to sound therapeutic.

If someone uses three of these in one conversation, evacuate.
You're in a cult meeting.

## Why "Circle Back" Is the Most Dangerous of Them All

Most jargon is annoying.
"Circle back" is destructive.

It sounds responsible.
It pretends to be accountable.
It feels like a plan.

But it is an empty promise dressed in khakis.


People who say it:
Don't remember,
Don't follow up,
Don't deliver,
Expect YOU to chase THEM.

They treat deadlines like folklore and accountability like a cryptid sighting.

And when you do follow up, they hit you with:

"Oh yeah - let's circle back on that."

Absolutely not.
We're not circling.
We're done.

If I wanted to chase people for answers, I'd become a kindergarten teacher.

## Why This Chapter Matters

Corporate jargon isn't just annoying. It's camouflage.
It's how people avoid responsibility while sounding like they're doing something important.
"Circle back" is the worst of them all because it pretends to be a plan when it's actually an escape hatch.

Every time someone says it, they're not committing.
They're not owning anything.
They're not agreeing to take action.
They're tossing the problem into the future and hoping Future You forgets it ever existed.

That's why this chapter matters.
Because the phrase isn't harmless.
It's a symptom of a workplace culture where clarity feels dangerous and accountability feels optional.
Where people talk in loops instead of lines.
Where entire projects stall because nobody wants to say the truth out loud.

"Circle back" survives because it's comfortable.
It lets people pretend they're collaborating while sidestepping every real decision.
It fills meetings, emails, and calendars with noise instead of substance.
And every one of us has sat through conversations where the only measurable output was another vague promise to "revisit later."

When language gets this slippery, work gets slower.
Communication gets murkier.
Ownership disappears.
And frustration climbs until you're questioning whether anyone in the room actually has a pulse.

So yes, it's just a phrase.
But it represents something bigger: the slow erosion of saying what we mean and doing what we say.

And every time someone drops a "let's circle back" to dodge responsibility, avoid commitment, or punt the problem into infinity, it becomes painfully obvious:

This is why we can't have nice things.

# CHAPTER 32 - Cheaters: The Art of Getting Ahead Without Earning It

There are certain people you meet in life who reveal everything you'll ever need to know about humanity - and none of it is good. For me, that person was a guy I'll call "Tyler," because that was his actual name, and I refuse to expend creative energy protecting a grown man who once cheated at Uno.

Tyler cheated at everything.
Not because he needed to.
Not because he was desperate.
Not because he was preventing global catastrophe via rogue trivia question.

Nope.

He cheated at board games.
He cheated at bar trivia.
He cheated at Fitbit step challenges - which is bold, because if you're shaking your wrist while eating Doritos, you're not tricking the Fitbit. You're tricking yourself.

He'd look around afterward like he'd just completed a covert CIA mission.

Buddy... nobody is awarding the Presidential Medal of Freedom for naming all the cast members of *Full House* in under ten seconds.

And as I've gotten older - and angrier - and more caffeinated - I've realized something:

The world is crawling with Tylers.

They multiply.
They swarm.
They travel in packs like pigeons, but significantly more shameless.

And every time one of them gets away with something, the rest of us pay the price.

That's the real damage.
Not the shortcut itself, but the way it teaches everyone else that honesty is for suckers.

This is why we can't have nice things.

Cheating isn't a moment.
It's a lifestyle.
A whole ecosystem of shortcuts, excuses, and wildly inflated self-esteem.

So let's take a tour through the many species of cheaters walking among us.

## Relationship Cheaters

Relationship cheaters genuinely believe they're starring in a low-budget spy thriller. Their phone lights up at midnight, they swan-dive across the couch to hide it, and somehow *you're* the one accused of "being paranoid."

I knew a guy - let's call him "Matt," because that's what it said on his Starbucks cup - who once claimed the lipstick on his collar came from "hugging a coworker."

Buddy, unless your coworker hugs like she's reenacting *The Notebook* during a hurricane, we both know what happened.

The mental gymnastics?
Olympic level.

Late-night texts were "work-related."
The secret Instagram was "for recipes."
Deleted call logs? "A glitch."

A glitch.
Right next to Bigfoot and UFO abductions.

The funniest part? They think they're subtle.

They're as subtle as a marching band sneaking into a library.

## Workplace Cheaters

Workplace cheaters treat the office like a multiplayer game where the goal is:

Do the least.
Collect the most.
Smile like a local newscaster.

I once worked with a guy - let's call him "Randy" - who volunteered for projects the way people volunteer for dental surgery. Yet when the hard part was done, he'd swoop in like a corporate vulture ready to feast on your accomplishments.

"Oh, let me send the final email!"
Translation: *I'd like full credit for this thing I barely understand.*

Their skill set is universal:
They know when free food arrives.
They know how to look stressed without doing anything.
They've mastered the "walk fast while holding a folder" maneuver - corporate camouflage at its finest.
They know when management is watching.
They know exactly how to attach themselves to your success like a barnacle with a 401(k).

Workplace cheaters are why everyone else needs a chiropractor.

## Parenting Cheaters

Parenting cheaters aren't helping their kids.
They're reliving the glory days they never had.

I once watched a mom brag her toddler "already knows three shapes."

Lady, they live in a world made of shapes. This isn't a Mensa qualifier.

Then there are the parents who cheat in children's games - blocking shots, checking their kid in flag football, screaming at referees like the fate of democracy depends on a second-grade soccer call.

But the worst offenders?
Parents who "assist" with school projects.

If your kid's papier-mâché volcano looks like it was produced by *Industrial Light & Magic*, we ALL know who earned that A.

That kid didn't build a solar system - he supervised it.

# Driving Cheaters

If you ever want to see cheating in its natural habitat, stand near a merge lane during rush hour.

Driving cheaters play the same script every time:

Ignore the entire line.
Floor it like they're outrunning an arrest warrant.
Cut in at the last second.
Act offended when someone honks.
Wave politely, as if that erases the crime.

One guy cut off forty cars, then looked personally wounded when someone refused to let him in. Like courtesy is a constitutional right.

Driving cheaters are why road rage exists.
Driving cheaters are why therapy exists.
Driving cheaters are why my blood pressure could power a small city.

Traffic isn't a natural disaster - it's man-made stupidity in motion.

# Gaming Cheaters

Gaming cheaters are the purest form of the species.
They cheat when NOTHING is at stake.

They unplug controllers, block the screen, insist the console is "lagging," or pause the game right before you win.

I once played Mario Kart with a guy who threw a pillow at the TV when he lost.
Not because he *was* cheated - because he *was cheating* and STILL lost.

That is a spiritual condition.

# Line-Cutting Cheaters

Line-cutting cheaters are the final evolutionary stage of shamelessness.

They walk past twenty patiently waiting humans, then slide into the front like they were summoned by God or the store manager.

A guy once tried to cut in front of me with two full carts and said:

"I'm in a hurry."

Congratulations, sir.
So is literally everyone else.

Lines exist because society does - barely.

# Because the Universe Never Stops Giving

Tyler wasn't the only specimen.

There was also a coworker I'll call "Jason," mostly because if I used his real name, he'd absolutely complain about "misrepresentation."

Jason once cheated in a workplace wellness challenge… by putting his Fitbit on his dog.

And the worst part?
The dog won.

Jason strutted around afterward like he'd completed a triathlon, conveniently ignoring the fact that his Labrador was the one doing cardio.

Someone congratulated him. He said:

"Thanks! I've been pushing myself."

Sure you have, Jason.
Right to the bottom of the dignity barrel.

This is why we can't have nice things.

## Cheaters Think They're Winning - They Aren't

Cheaters think they're geniuses.
They think the rest of us are suckers.
They think they've unlocked a secret life hack the honest people are too "square" to use.

But everyone else sees exactly what they are:

Sloppy.
Transparent.
Exhausting.
Embarrassing.
Always sweating for no good reason.

Cheaters aren't getting ahead.
They're just burning the world's patience one shortcut at a time.

## Why This Chapter Matters

Cheaters make life harder for everyone who's just trying to survive adulthood with their sanity intact.

Every time a cheater skips a line, steals credit, avoids consequences, or lies badly, *you* end up carrying the cost - in time, in patience, in faith that people aren't exhausting by default.

Cheaters aren't proof the world is unfair in big dramatic ways. They're proof the world is unfair in a thousand stupid, mundane, sanity-eroding ways.

And that's exactly the kind of daily nonsense this book exists to expose.

You're not pissed off for no reason.
You're pissed off because you're surrounded by people treating life like a loophole scavenger hunt while you're over here doing things the adult way - the way it's supposed to be done.

Cheaters don't just cut corners.
They cut your patience.
They cut your time.
They cut your faith in humanity down to the nub.

And every time one of these shortcut-loving, Fitbit-strapping, Mario-Kart-pausing clowns gets away with something, the rest of us lose one more sliver of peace.

Which is exactly why - say it with me -

This is why we can't have nice things.

**PART IV - WHAT WE CAN ACTUALLY DO ABOUT IT**
Because being pissed off is valid - but staying pissed off forever will kill you.

# CHAPTER 33 - How Not to Lose Your Mind in a Ridiculous World

There comes a moment in adulthood when you realize the world isn't going to get less stupid. There's never going to be a morning where you wake up to a breaking-news alert saying:

"Humanity has decided to stop being irritating."

Nope.

Instead, you wake up to a fresh buffet of nonsense:
a subscription charge you definitely did not sign up for,
a text message the length of a biblical scroll,
three corporations begging you to take a survey about something you bought half-asleep at 7 a.m..

The world isn't just ridiculous - it is relentlessly ridiculous.

And every day, the universe wakes up and says,
"Oh good, you're conscious. Here are twelve new things specifically designed to test your remaining patience."

Unless you build defenses, you will eventually end up on a viral TikTok screaming at a gas pump because it beeped at you twice.

This chapter isn't about "self-care."

It's about survival - the kind that prevents you from spontaneously combusting in Target.

Because if adulthood has taught me anything, it's that inner peace is a myth sold by people who don't answer emails.

## Managing Frustration Without Developing an Eye Twitch

Being pissed off is normal.
Being overwhelmed is normal.
Feeling like the world is a badly written sitcom is absolutely normal.

But adulthood requires a system - a way to sort the nonsense worth caring about from the nonsense you should punt directly into the sun.

People think maturity is about patience.
Wrong.

Maturity is knowing which stupid things deserve your energy.

Some systems are built to frustrate you.
Some people exist solely to annoy you.
Some interactions are emotional booby traps.

So it's time to build your mental toolbox.

## The Essential Toolkit for Surviving Daily Bullshit

Every adult needs emotional utilities - tools you can summon like a pissed-off Batman.

### The Deep Sigh
A powerful exhale that communicates:
"I am trying very hard not to end up on a watchlist."

It's the universal sound of a human rebooting after witnessing stupidity in the wild.

### The Middle-Aged Eye Roll
Not the subtle kind - the full-rotation, orbital shift.
If you do it right, someone nearby will ask if you're okay.
You are not.

### The "Nope, Not Today" Walk-Away
Your body takes over and escorts you out before your mouth says something HR will laminate.

### Emotional Airplane Mode
Not responding.
Not engaging.
Not caring.
You are a human screenshot with the WiFi turned off.
It's not avoidance - it's emotional battery-saving mode.

### The Internal "What the Hell Is Wrong With People?" Monologue
Silent. Judgy. Cleansing.
A mental palate cleanser for idiots.

## Avoiding Burnout When the World Refuses to Shut Up

Burnout isn't exhaustion - it's irritation collapse.

It's when you've been annoyed for so long you no longer have the energy to be annoyed.

Like the day I spent 37 minutes arguing with a toaster.

Every push of the lever was a personal attack.

At minute 20, I was furious.
At minute 30, I felt myself dying.
At minute 37, I whispered, "Fine. Win."

That's not acceptance - that's defeat.

Burnout happens when your ability to care gets beaten to death by repetition.

It's death by a thousand annoyances - not one big breakdown, just cumulative stupidity wearing you down like emotional sandpaper.

You need breaks. Not spa retreats - just emotional step-backs:
turn off notifications,
mute exhausting people,
refuse pointless arguments,
walk away from stupidity early.

There are no trophies for staying engaged with every irritation.

## Learning to Disengage Without Becoming Detached

Disengagement isn't weakness.
Disengagement is strategy.

You do NOT have to:
answer every text,
debate every idiot,
join every group conversation,
correct every wrong thing someone says online.

Sometimes the strongest move is silence.

Silence is powerful.

Silence is peaceful.
Silence is the only thing stopping you from explaining basic logic to someone who thinks turn signals are optional.

You can't control stupid people, broken systems, or companies that think "convenience fee" is a cute phrase.

But you *can* control what gets access to your mental space.

## A Costco Story of Spiritual Awakening

One time, a man cut in front of me at a Costco sample table - for a microwaved taco bite that looked like a science experiment.

I tapped him and said, "There's a line."

He turned and replied:
"Relax. It's free."

And something inside me… broke.

I realized I was seconds away from debating this man over a 23-cent meat cube.
That was my enlightenment moment.

I walked away.
Not because he was right.
But because he wasn't worth the emotional calories.

That's sanity.
That's survival.
That's choosing YOU.

# The Cultural Plague of Toxic Positivity

Let's talk about one of the most exhausting forces on Earth: people who weaponize positivity.

Your job is killing you?

"Smile more!"

Your bills doubled?

"Manifest abundance!"

Your toddler threw a waffle at your face?

"Practice gratitude!"

These are the same people who chirp:

"Everything happens for a reason!"

Yes. The reason is usually that someone else screwed up.

Positivity is fine.

Forced positivity is emotional gaslighting with glitter.

And these are the same people who act shocked when you're stressed - as if adulthood isn't just a series of invoices, micro-annoyances, and mild disappointments.

# Sanity Isn't Perfection - It's Boundaries

You need boundaries that can survive a category-five stupidity hurricane.

Say:
"No."
"Not today."
"I'm busy."
"I don't care."
"Leave me alone."
"I'm muting this chat for the next eight hours."

Boundaries protect your peace from the world's nonsense.

Once you master boundaries - once you embrace frustration, manage energy, disengage early, and reject fake optimism - the world doesn't magically improve...

...but you get harder to rattle.

Because at some point, you realize you're not fighting the world - you're just dodging the people determined to make it worse one annoying interaction at a time.

And that, my friend, is how you keep your mind intact in a world actively trying to break it.

Because honestly?

If the world had a return policy, most of us would've exchanged it by now.

This is why we can't have nice things.

## Why This Chapter Matters

This chapter isn't about inner peace, mindfulness, or becoming the kind of person who journals about gratitude at sunrise.

It's about survival.

Because the world isn't getting quieter, calmer, or more reasonable. It's getting louder, dumber, and more exhausting - one notification, one inconvenience, one human interaction at a time.

Adulthood isn't hard because of the big things.
It's hard because of the relentless parade of small, stupid things that chip away at your sanity until you start having heated arguments with appliances.

Learning how to stay sane in a ridiculous world matters because nobody teaches you how.
Nobody hands you a manual.
Nobody says, "Hey, here's how to not lose your composure while standing behind someone writing a check at the grocery store in 2025."

This chapter exists because frustration is universal.
Because burnout is real.
Because everyone is one inconvenience away from snapping at a self-checkout machine.

And because once you understand that your sanity depends on boundaries, disengagement, and the courage to not care about every stupid thing the world throws at you…

…life gets lighter.

Not easier - just less likely to make you scream into a steering wheel.

If this book has a heartbeat, it's this:

You're not overreacting.
You're not dramatic.

You're not "too sensitive."

The world *is* ridiculous.

And every time you choose to protect your peace instead of diving face-first into the madness, you take back a little bit of your sanity in a world determined to steal it.

Which is exactly why -

This is why we can't have nice things.

# CHAPTER 34 - Stoicism for Pissed-Off People

There's a point in adulthood where you realize the world isn't calming down.
It's not stabilizing.
It's not maturing.
It's not "finding itself."

No - it's doubling down on nonsense.

People are filming TikTok's in bathroom stalls.
Corporate printers still jam like it's their religion.
Every app wants your email, phone number, birthday, and possibly a blood sample.
Someone, right now, is microwaving fish at work.

And if you're not careful, this slow drip of stupidity will eventually break you.

That's why we need Stoicism - not the toga version, the modern survival version - the kind that keeps you from screaming into a pillow until your neighbors call for a wellness check.

Stoicism isn't about being calm.
It's about not losing your mind when the world absolutely deserves it.

It is, essentially, emotional deodorant for everyday irritation.

# Stoicism Without All the Ancient Homework

Let's define Stoicism in terms that don't require a college elective:

Stoicism is the discipline of caring only about what you can actually control…
and refusing to donate emotional energy to the things you can't.

It's not pretending everything's fine.
It's not "good vibes only."
It's not becoming so Zen that you float out of meetings on a cloud.

It's simply:

"I acknowledge the bullshit.
I'm just not letting the bullshit run my day."

You're not calm because you're spiritual.
You're calm because jail time is wildly inconvenient.

# Modern Stoicism: The Pissed-Off Edition

Ancient Stoics didn't have WiFi, HOA boards, or a self-checkout machine that accuses them of shoplifting every two minutes.
We need updated rules.

### Rule One: You Control You
Not the weather.
Not gas prices.
Not Karen in the parking lot.
Not your WiFi dropping right before a Zoom meeting.

Just you.

### Rule Two: Acceptance Isn't Approval
You don't have to like the DMV.
You just don't let the DMV become your villain origin story.

### Rule Three: Choose Your Battles
You don't need to correct every idiot.
You don't need to win every argument.
You don't need to emotionally invest in every inconvenience.

If the hill is stupid, don't die on it.

### Rule Four: Expect the Stupidity
If you anticipate nonsense, you can't be blindsided by it.
It's not pessimism - it's emotional insurance.

## Stoicism Isn't Passive - It's Tactical

People confuse Stoicism with rolling over. No.

Stoicism is strategy.
It's emotional aikido.
It's picking where your sanity goes - and where it doesn't.

Stoicism sounds like:
"I could get angry... but why would I waste bandwidth on this clown?"

It's not detachment.
It's efficiency.

## The TSA Incident That Tested My Soul

One time, I tried to practice Stoicism in an airport - a place specifically engineered to destroy human patience.

I stayed calm.
I breathed.
I accepted reality.

Then TSA pulled me aside, opened my backpack, and discovered a forgotten sandwich.

They handled that sandwich like it was radioactive.
They tested it for explosives.
They held it up to the light like it was forged in Mordor.

My turkey sandwich received more federal attention than half the luggage in that building.

And that…
was the moment my Stoicism briefly died.

But that's the point - Stoicism doesn't mean perfection.
It means doing your best while surrounded by situations that frankly do not deserve your best.

## Mini Stoic Survival Guide for Adults Hanging On by a Thread

You don't need quotes, scrolls, marble busts, or a philosophy degree.

You just need three phrases:

"I don't control this."
"It's not worth it."
"Not today."

Say them early, say them often, say them before you end up screaming at an inanimate object in public.
Because you will face nonsense.

You will face incompetence.
You will face humans behaving like they were raised by malfunctioning vending machines.

But Stoicism lets you walk away intact.

## Why This Chapter Matters

Because staying sane is a full-time job in a world that keeps trying to recruit you into madness.

Stoicism isn't about becoming peaceful - it's about protecting your energy from the daily parade of stupidity you didn't sign up for. It's what keeps you from arguing with strangers, losing your temper over microwaved fish, or letting someone else's chaos hijack your entire day.

This chapter matters because it gives you permission to stop pouring emotional fuel into every ridiculous situation. It reminds you that you don't have to react to everything, fix everything, or absorb every annoyance thrown your way.

Some battles aren't worth fighting.
Some people aren't worth correcting.
Some nonsense isn't worth your pulse.

And when you hold that boundary -
when you save your patience instead of spending it -
you regain the one thing adulthood keeps trying to steal:

your peace.

Which is exactly why, in a world as exhausting as this one...

This is why we can't have nice things.

# CHAPTER 35 - Choosing Your Battles (Even When You Want to Fight All of Them)

There comes a point in adulthood where you realize life is basically one long parade of battles - some big, some small, and some so stupid you feel personally insulted they even crossed your path.

And if you're the type who gets pissed off easily (which means you're normal), your instinct is to fight *every* single one of them - even the ones that only exist because someone else's brain is running on airplane mode.

Here's the uncomfortable truth:

If you fight every battle, you'll die exhausted, bitter, and probably mid-rant at a cashier who is just trying to get through her shift.

Not every hill is worth dying on.
Some hills aren't even hills - they're speed bumps created by idiots.

This chapter is about the art of picking your battles - a skill that will save your sanity, your time, your blood pressure, and probably your criminal record.

## Not Every Hill Is Worth Dying On (Even If You Really Want It To Be)

There are battles that genuinely matter...

...and then there are battles that only matter to the angrier, pettier version of you who lives two inches under your sternum.

**Worth fighting:**
Someone disrespected you.
Someone violated your boundary.
Someone endangered you.
Someone lied about you.
Someone is taking advantage of you.
A system is screwing you on purpose.

**Not worth fighting:**
A stranger is wrong on the internet.
Someone says "irregardless."
The car in front of you didn't use a blinker.
Your coworker smacks their lips while eating yogurt.
A teenager calls you "bruh."
A barista spells your name "Mary" with a 'y' instead of an 'i'.
The person ahead of you is paying in pennies from the Eisenhower administration.

Your outrage wants to fight them all.
Your sanity begs you not to.

You only have so many fucks to give.
Spend them wisely.

## Battles Absolutely Not Worth Fighting Under Any Circumstance

Some battles are so pointless they should come with a biohazard label: Arguing with anyone who uses Facebook as their primary news source. If their profile picture is a wolf, an eagle, or a Minion meme, walk away.
Fighting over a parking spot in a parking lot full of parking spots.

Debating someone who says "I did my own research." No you didn't, Randy.
Explaining science to someone who thinks WiFi causes knee pain.
Trying to reason with anyone wearing pajama pants in public after 2 p.m. They've surrendered; you should too.
Correcting a stranger's grammar online. They will type worse out of spite.
Any argument that begins with "As a mother…" or "As an empath…" You've already lost.

You will not win these battles.
You will not break even.
You will not leave with dignity.

The house always wins - and in this case, the house is stupidity.

## How to Avoid Pointless Arguments (Especially the Ones You're Dying to Win)

Some arguments are irresistible.

You see the wrongness, the ignorance, the pure uncut stupidity - and your whole nervous system screams:

"I HAVE TO SAY SOMETHING."

Listen carefully:

You will never win an argument with someone who enjoys being wrong.

Pointless arguments usually involve:
someone arguing from insecurity,
someone arguing for attention,
someone arguing out of boredom,

someone who treats ignorance like a personality trait.

Arguing with these people is like teaching algebra to a potato.
You waste your time, you waste your energy, and the potato learns nothing.

Online, it's worse.

You think it's a conversation.
They think it's the Super Bowl.

You reply once and suddenly 17 women named Diane are in your mentions telling you to "educate yourself."

Memorize this:

"I don't have to respond."

## Internal Battles vs. External Battles

External battles are obvious.
You point at the chaos and say, "This. This right here is why society is failing. This is why we can't have nice things."

Internal battles are trickier. They happen at 1 a.m., when you replay a conversation and mentally rewrite it with better comebacks.

Internal battles include:
fighting the urge to clap back,
fighting the need to "fix" every idiot,
fighting the compulsion to overexplain,
fighting the itch to respond to that text immediately,
fighting the fantasy of saying exactly what you want, consequences be damned.

Internal battles drain you silently.
No witnesses.
No applause.
No medals.

But they matter more than any external war you'll ever face.

Controlling your internal battles is how you control your external reactions.

## A Story of Choosing the Wrong Battle

Once, I chose the wrong battle - gloriously, publicly, stupidly.

A guy at a gas station parked diagonally across two spots like he was recreating a crime scene diagram.

I said, "Nice parking job."
He said, "Mind your own business."

Reason left my body.

What began as a throwaway comment became a 12-minute argument where we gestured at asphalt like we were debating the Constitution.

Did he move? No.
Did anything change? No.
Did I feel better? Also no.

Later I realized:

That wasn't a battle.
That was cardio with yelling.

# A Moment When Choosing the Right Battle Saved Me

Then there was the time I was behind a woman with 22 items in the 10-items-or-less lane.

Old me would have died on that hill.

New me said:

"Nope. You're not worth a day of serotonin."

I walked out.
Ordered groceries delivered.
Paid the extra fee.

And you know what?

Sanity is always worth the surcharge.

# The Battle Triage System

If you're unsure whether to engage, run it through this cheap but wildly effective filter:

**Step 1:** Will this matter in five minutes?
If no → disengage.

**Step 2:** Will engaging improve anything?
If no → disengage faster.

**Step 3:** Is this person capable of shame, logic, or accountability?
If no → run.

**Step 4:** Will fighting this make you feel better tomorrow?
If no → your ego is baiting you.

**Step 5:** Is this worth explaining to a judge?
If no → walk away immediately.
If maybe → also walk away.
If yes → proceed with caution.

This little framework will save more sanity than half the meditation apps on the market.

## The Real Art of Choosing Your Battles

Choosing your battles isn't weakness - it's power.

It's not avoiding conflict.
It's avoiding *stupid* conflict.

It's the difference between being controlled by your anger and being in command of it.

Choosing your battles protects:

your peace,
your time,
your mental bandwidth,
your rapidly dwindling patience.

The world offers infinite opportunities to explode.
You don't have to accept every invitation.

When you finally master the art of choosing your battles?

You unlock something dangerously rare:

peace...
in a world that gives you every reason to lose it.

Naturally...

This is why we can't have nice things.

## Why This Chapter Matters

Choosing your battles isn't about being calm, or enlightened, or spiritually evolved.
It's about survival.
Because if you try to fight every stupid, irritating, soul-draining moment thrown at you, the world will eat you alive before lunch.

Life isn't one big war.
It's a thousand tiny skirmishes designed to trick you into wasting your energy on nonsense:

the guy blocking the cereal aisle,
the stranger wrong on the internet,
the driver who treats turn signals like ancient folklore.

If you don't learn how to filter what deserves your fire and what deserves your silence, you end up drained, angry, and muttering threats in the produce section.

This chapter matters because choosing your battles is how you protect what's left of your sanity.
It's how you reclaim your time.
It's how you stop letting idiots reroute your entire emotional day.

You are not obligated to engage every provocation.
You're not required to educate everyone.
You're not responsible for correcting society one argument at a time.

Your energy is limited.
The world's stupidity is not.

And that is exactly why knowing which fights to skip is one of the few ways to stay functional in a world that seems determined to push every button you have.

Because once you learn how to walk away without guilt, without second-guessing, without choosing violence over peace?

You suddenly understand, with painful clarity:

This is why we can't have nice things.

# CHAPTER 36 - Finding Humor in the Absurd

There's a moment in adulthood - usually somewhere between your third customer service call of the week and your fifteenth "Sorry, we're short-staffed" - when you realize something important:

If you don't learn to laugh at the absurdity around you, you're going to lose your entire mind.

Not metaphorically.
Not dramatically.
Literally.

You will snap like a Costco rotisserie chicken.

And honestly, some days it feels like the only thing holding you together is spite and whatever caffeine you can legally obtain.

Modern life isn't just stressful - it's unintentionally hilarious. The world is so stupid, so chaotic, so poorly managed by the collective IQ of a damp sponge, that the only sane reaction left is laughter.

Comedy isn't a distraction.
It's a coping mechanism.
It's emotional duct tape for a world held together by malfunctioning apps, inconsistent signage, and the collective decision to ignore common sense.
It's emotional armor made of sarcasm and bad timing.

You're not laughing because it's all okay.
You're laughing because the alternative is burning down a Walmart.

# Comedy as Survival

People talk about "finding joy" like it's a craft project you can order on Etsy.
Joy is fragile. Joy needs to be nurtured.

Humor, though?

Humor is feral.
Humor survives in the wild.
Humor will crawl out of the rubble after everything else is gone.

Humor is the cockroach of human emotions - it outlives everything.

You don't "find" humor by accident.
You choose it.

Stupid thing happens, you get a choice:
internalize it and stew, or
convert it into comedy like an emotional recycling plant.

Someone cuts you off? Comedy.
Someone says "I was hacked" after posting something stupid? Comedy.
Someone watches one YouTube video and declares themselves an expert? Comedy.

If you don't laugh, you rage.
Rage long enough and you burn out.
Burn out long enough and you start muttering to yourself in public.

And that's when you become the neighborhood legend:
"Don't stare, Timmy. That's the man who fought the parking meter."

So yes, humor is therapy.

It's also resistance.

It's your way of saying:

"You cannot break me. I already think you're ridiculous."

And once you accept that humor is survival, not decoration, something clicks.

## Turning Frustration Into Stories (The Only Reward Modern Life Gives You)

One of the most healing things you can do with your frustration is turn it into a story.

Stories are power.
They reframe the chaos.
They turn the worst moments into something you can at least use.

You know that moment when something infuriating happens and, even as you're seething, a tiny voice in your head whispers:

"…Okay, but this is gonna be a great story later."

On hold for 57 minutes?
Story.

Neighbor blasting EDM at 2 a.m.?
Story.

Self-checkout screaming "UNEXPECTED ITEM IN THE BAGGING AREA" like a hostile robot?
Story.

Life gives you rage.

You turn it into stand-up material.

That's how emotionally stable adults avoid federal charges.

Some stories are funny by dinner.
Some take years.
Some need three therapy sessions before you can tell them without twitching.

But storytelling makes frustration useful.
It's emotional compost: bitterness becomes fuel.

And people love these stories, because everyone has lived some version of them.

Shared frustration is bonding.
Shared stupidity is community.
Shared comedy is healing.

## The Healing Power of Laughing at Idiots

Let's be very clear:

Laughing at idiots is good for your health.

Not bullying. Not cruelty. Not punching down.
Just acknowledging that the world is full of people doing gloriously dumb things and choosing to laugh instead of fight.

There is real spiritual relief in looking at a situation and thinking:

"My God… you're ridiculous."

Idiots are everywhere:
people who can't merge,

people who quote TikTok as "research,"
people who brag about being "alpha males,"
people who ask questions during movies,
people who bring tuna sandwiches to a sauna,
people who tell cashiers "It scanned twice, but I'll just take the extra one,"
people who microwave fish at work (Chapter 28, your legacy is secure).

Idiots are a renewable resource.

If you treat every idiot like a personal challenge, you'll die of exhaustion.
If you treat them like background characters in a dark comedy, you'll live longer.

## Absurd Situations Every Adult Experiences

Proof that we're all barely holding it together:

**The mystery wet spot on the grocery store floor.**
No one knows what it is. No one asks. Everyone tiptoes around it like it's radioactive.

**The customer screaming at a cashier while being objectively wrong.**
They argue louder, not smarter.

**The coworker who reheats fish and says, "Smells fine to me."**
Your nose is lying to you, Debra.

**The person who parks their cart sideways in the busiest aisle and then just... thinks.**
Move or perish.

**The person filming vertical video at a funeral.**
Humanity is on backorder.

Every one of these moments can ruin your day - or be the funniest thing you've seen all week, depending on how you decide to file it.

## A Brief Heartfelt Moment: Why Humor Actually Matters

Here's the part nobody tells you as a kid:

Life gets heavy.

People disappoint you.
Systems fail you.
Stress turns into background radiation.

I figured out early - way before this book existed - that humor is what keeps you from sinking.

It doesn't erase the hard stuff.
It doesn't magically fix anything.

But it gives you breathing room.
It turns "I can't do this" into "Okay… I can at least laugh about this later."

Finding humor isn't minimizing pain.
It's refusing to drown in it.

You don't laugh because life is easy.
You laugh because life is absurd.

# The Gas Station Burrito Meltdown

One morning, I watched a man absolutely implode at a gas station because the microwave was "taking too long" to heat his burrito.

He slammed the microwave door.
He barked at the clerk:

"I HAVE PLACES TO BE!"

Then he stormed out.

Without the burrito.

He left his entire breakfast behind like it had betrayed him.

I stood there, stunned… and then I started laughing. Not polite laughter - full-body, can't-hold-it-in laughing.

That meltdown reset my entire day.

His tragedy.
My emotional reboot.

That's humor.
That's survival.

# The Banana Incident

Another time, I watched a man come emotionally unglued in the produce section because he couldn't separate a bunch of bananas.

He tugged once. Nothing.
Tugged twice. Still nothing.
On the third tug, he broke.

He let out this exhausted, defeated groan and whispered:

"Why is everything so HARD?!"

He wasn't just talking about the bananas.
You could tell this was about everything.

Work. Bills. Life. All of it.
The bananas were just the final boss.

And there I was, ten feet away, trying so hard not to laugh loud enough to get escorted out of the store.

And the thing is, that moment wasn't just funny - it was clarifying.
Humor shows up exactly when your patience taps out.

That moment carried me emotionally for a week.

## Humor Makes the Absurd Bearable

At the end of the day:
the world will still be stupid,
people will still be ridiculous,
systems will still be broken,
and somebody, somewhere, will still be microwaving fish.

Humor doesn't fix any of that.

But it makes the absurd bearable.
It turns chaos into catharsis.
It turns irritation into relief.

You don't laugh because you're above it.
You laugh because you refuse to let it crush you.

Humor doesn't fix the world -
but it absolutely changes your experience of living in it.

And even when everything feels broken…

This is why we can't have nice things -
but at least we can laugh about it.

## Why This Chapter Matters

Life isn't getting less ridiculous.
People aren't getting wiser.
Systems aren't getting smoother.
If anything, the absurdity is scaling like a bad subscription service.

And when the world gets louder, dumber, and more exhausting, you only have two choices:

Break…
or laugh.

Humor is how you stay upright when everything around you is wobbling.
It's how you take a moment that should ruin your day and turn it into a story instead.

Finding the absurd isn't denial.
It's protection.
It keeps the stupid from sinking its hooks too deep.

Because the truth is simple:
You can't control how ridiculous people are.
You can't fix every mess.
You can't debate every idiot.

You can't even trust the self-checkout not to scream at you.

But you *can* control how much of your peace you sacrifice.

Humor gives you that control.
It gives you distance.
It gives you leverage over the nonsense.

It turns irritation into oxygen.
It turns chaos into something survivable.
It turns "I'm losing my mind" into "Okay… that was insane, but at least it's funny now."

And when everything feels heavy, ridiculous, or aggressively stupid, humor is what lets you keep going without turning into the person who yells at a barista because the lid isn't on straight.

Laughing at the absurd doesn't fix the world.
But it fixes *your* ability to live in it.

Which is exactly why -
say it with me -

this is why we can't have nice things.

# CHAPTER 37 - The Surprisingly Rewarding Art of Not Giving a Damn

At some point in adulthood, a quiet miracle happens.
Not a spiritual awakening.
Not a come-to-Jesus moment.
Not even one of those "new year, new me" delusions we tell ourselves every January.

No - you simply wake up one morning and realize…

you don't have enough damns left to give.

They're gone.
Depleted.
Evaporated like hope at the DMV.

And instead of panicking, you feel peace.
Real peace.
The kind of peace that should require a prescription.

For years, you cared - about everything.
People's opinions.
Strangers' comments.
Coworkers' nonsense.
Random crises the news told you to be upset about.
Group chats you didn't even want to be in.

Then one day… something inside you snapped.
But in a good way.

The "give-a-damn" tank finally hit empty, and your whole body exhaled like it had been holding its breath since 2008.

It's the closest thing adulthood has to enlightenment - the moment your brain whispers, "We're done here," and refuses to load any more nonsense.

Welcome to the art of not giving a damn - one of adulthood's only legitimate upgrades.

## The Magic of Selective Caring

Not giving a damn isn't apathy.
(It's not sociopathy - we'll leave that to your ex.)

It's selective caring.
Strategic caring.
Choosing what actually deserves your emotional calories.

You start asking three life-changing questions:

Does this actually matter?
Does this affect my life in any meaningful way?
Is this worth one of my precious remaining damns?

If the answer to all three is no?
Congratulations - you are free.

Someone's offended you didn't reply in 14 minutes?
Nope.

Coworker wants you to passionately care about Q3 alignment charts?
Absolutely not.

A stranger online tells you your opinion is wrong?

Hold, please, while I check my inventory of damns...
...ah. Still zero.

## The Peace That Comes From Boundaries

One of the great joys of adulthood is learning that boundaries aren't rude - they're survival.

"No."
"Not today."
"I'm unavailable."
"That's a you problem."

These words unlock a peace previously reserved for monks and people who delete Facebook.

Boundaries don't push people away - they push nonsense away.

And yes, some people will get offended when you stop letting them drain your energy like emotional mosquitos.
But their discomfort is not your concern.

If someone doesn't like your boundaries, that's just proof they benefitted from you not having any.

Boundaries are the security system for your sanity.

## The Freedom of Letting People Judge You

People will judge you no matter what.

Care too much?
"Try-hard."

Care too little?
"Aloof."

Set boundaries?
"Selfish."

Be available?
"Too nice."

You cannot win.
The game is rigged.

So stop playing.

When you finally stop managing the emotions of people who contribute nothing to your life, you become unstoppable.
You walk differently.
You breathe differently.
You radiate the energy of someone with maybe six damns left for the entire month - and today isn't the day any of them get used.

## The Time You Get Back Is Unreal

When you stop giving a damn about the wrong things, suddenly you have:
more time,
more peace,
more mental space,
more emotional bandwidth,
more clarity,
more "who gives a shit?" freedom.

Most of what you used to worry about either:
never mattered,
stopped mattering,

or wasn't yours to carry in the first place.

Half the stuff that haunted you five years ago?

Gone.
Dust.
Irrelevant.

## The Day I Officially Ran Out of Damns

The day I realized my damns were gone wasn't dramatic.

It was a staff meeting.

Someone put up a slide titled "Synergizing Team-Based Holistic Outcomes."
Corporate for: "Prepare to waste the next hour of your life."

Three minutes in, someone asked a question so irrelevant it could be used for psychological interrogation.

I felt my soul leave my body.
Just float up, wave, and go find a drink.

But instead of rage…
I felt nothing.
Peaceful, glorious nothing.

Because I truly did not give a single damn.

Nothing around me changed.
I changed - because I stopped donating emotional energy to things that didn't deserve it.

# Because Adulthood Never Stops Providing Material

Another time, a neighbor knocked on my door to inform me my recycling bin was - and I quote - "emotionally aggressive."

I blinked.
He blinked.

And that was it.
That was the exact moment I realized I had officially retired from giving a damn about neighborhood theatrics.

My bin wasn't the problem.
His need for something to complain about was.

And I wasn't signing up for that subscription.

# Things I No Longer Give a Damn About

People who walk slowly in grocery aisles.
Anyone who says "we need to circle back."
Online strangers debating me like I'm on CNN.
Family members demanding explanations for my boundaries.
Dishwasher "critics."
Celebrities giving motivational speeches from mansions.
People who microwave fish.
Corporate emails that end with "Warmly."
"We need to talk."
Stores asking for my email to buy a broom.
People who say "Just playing devil's advocate" like the devil needs an intern.

Every time you cross something off your list, you get a piece of your life back.

## The Emotional Detox of Not Giving a Damn

When you stop caring about the trivial, your whole system resets.

You sleep better.
You stress less.
You laugh more.
You disengage faster.
You stop being manipulated.
You stop taking everything personally.
You learn the magic of "Nope."

It's like your brain gets a software update.
Suddenly, nothing sticks.

Annoyances slide off you like water off a greased bowling ball.

Someone tries to drag you into a fight?
Not today.

Someone dumps their emotional laundry on you?
Return to sender.

Someone wants you to lose your peace over something stupid?
Absolutely not.

Your energy becomes yours again.

## The Ultimate Realization

Nobody tells you this in your 20s:

You don't have to attend every argument you're invited to.
You don't have to care about every opinion thrown your way.
You don't have to fix anything that isn't yours.
You don't owe emotional labor to everyone.
You don't have to prove anything to people who don't matter.

Not giving a damn isn't giving up.
It's leveling up.

## Why This Chapter Matters

Because adulthood is full of people, systems, expectations, and obligations begging for your attention - and most of them don't deserve it.

Because you only get so much energy each day, and wasting it on trivial nonsense is how you burn out without ever accomplishing anything meaningful.

Because the world will always demand more than it gives.
And unless you learn to protect your peace, you'll drown in obligations that were never yours to carry.

Because selective caring is freedom.
Boundaries are power.
And choosing where your energy goes is one of the few things in life you can actually control.

Because once you realize you don't owe the world unlimited access to your mind, your time, or your sanity...

You get your life back.

And every time you walk away from pointless chaos with your peace intact?

That's victory.
That's progress.
That's adulthood done right.

And honestly?

This is why we can't have nice things - but at least now you finally don't care.

# CONCLUSION - You're Not Wrong for Being Pissed Off

If you've made it to the end of this book, let me give you the validation society keeps acting like you don't deserve:

You're not crazy.
You're not dramatic.
You're not "too sensitive."
You're not overreacting.

You're paying attention.

Modern life is a full-time assault on your patience.
The world keeps handing you stress like it's a Costco sample:
forms,
fees,
phone trees,
deadlines,
password resets,
corporate nonsense,
and someone reheating fish in a shared microwave like they're waging biological warfare.

And somehow, you're expected to stay serene?
Grateful?
Grounded?

Please.

You're irritated because the world is irritating.
You're frustrated because the world is frustrating.

You're out of patience because everything demands your patience like it's a subscription service you never signed up for.

And yet… here you are.
Still functional(ish).
Still showing up.
Still trying to be a person while surrounded by people who clearly skipped the tutorial level of life.

Your fuse is short because the world keeps lighting it.
Not because you're broken - because you're awake.

Your frustration isn't failure.
It's proof you haven't gone numb.

It means you still give a damn about the right things -
even while learning not to give a damn about the wrong ones.

You're allowed to draw boundaries.
You're allowed to choose your battles.
You're allowed to protect your peace like it's an endangered species.
You're allowed to laugh at the absurdity instead of letting it bury you alive.

Life is stupid.
People are weird.
Systems are broken.
And everyone somehow thinks you're the unreasonable one for noticing.

But here's the truth nobody ever says out loud:

You're not the problem.
You're the witness.

You see the chaos clearly.

You feel the impact honestly.
You respond like someone who still has a pulse and a brain cell.

That's not negativity - that's awareness.

So take this book with you like emotional WD-40:
the thing that keeps you from rusting shut in a world determined to grind your gears into fine emotional powder.

You're not alone.
You're not wrong.
You're not "too much."
You're just done pretending nonsense is normal.

And that, honestly, is heroic these days.

So remember the one universal truth that ties every chapter, every rant, every eye twitch, every absurdity, and every ounce of your sanity together:

**This is why we can't have nice things.**

And thank God for that -
because at least it gives us something to laugh about.

www.ingramcontent.com/pod-product-compliance
Lightning Source LLC
LaVergne TN
LVHW042250070526
838201LV00089B/105